I0052684

IGNITE YOUR
DONOR PASSION

A ministryTHRIVE Production

© 2018 by John D. Leavy

All rights reserved.

Reproduction or translation of any part of this work beyond that permitted by Section 107 or 108 of the 1976 United States Copyright Act without permission of the copyright owner is unlawful. Requests for permission or further information should be emailed to: John D. Leavy at johndleavy@gmail.com.

This publication is designed to provide accurate and authoritative information regarding the subject matter covered. It is sold with the understanding that the publisher or author is not engaged in rendering legal, accounting, or other professional services. If legal advice or other expert assistance is required, the services of a competent professional person should be sought.

ISBN-13:

978-0692992586 (John D. Leavy)

ISBN-10:

0692992588

1st Printing 2017, 2019, 2nd Edition 2025

Printed in the United States of America

"I've seen you move
You have moved mountains
And I believe
I'll see you do it again"
Elevation Workshop

Contents

The Preface

C ommunicating with supporters and donors is the lifeblood of ministry. It's what makes every non-profit viable, invaluable, sustainable, and successful. It's not crass to mutter to oneself that "*ministry takes money*." It's how this world operates. It takes money to feed the poor, house the impoverished, drill wells in West Africa, start microbusinesses in Congo, raise someone's quality of life, or bring the Good News to unheard-of ears.

Conversing with supporters and donors is not a communicative dance whereby an organization works to position itself in a favorable light with an individual so that financial support can be secured.

Communicating with supporters and donors must be seen as a privilege, an honor, an opportunity, and finally as an occasion to begin to shape a life-long, mutual relationship of passion, support, and trust—an organization and an individual yoked in a common cause to make someone else's life situation better here on earth and eternally.

Ignite Your Donor Passion begins by identifying the five goals effective communication accomplishes: it informs, educates, engages, inspires, and causes action on the part of the recipient.

Ignite Your Donor Passion then discusses thirteen ingredients that contribute to the success of the communication between "the writer" and "the recipient.". The writer needs to reveal some personality when writing, offering insights into who they are and why they have taken on the work. The communication methods, regardless of the approach, must be donor-centric. The line of communication should first focus on building relationships, not the needs of the organization. The writer must always be blatantly honest. The calls for support, whether financial or physical, should be clear, concise, and obvious.

The stories being told must convey the impact the organization is having and how lives are being changed. If needs are lacking, then a sense of urgency must be expressed and explained.

The remaining portion of the first section deals with answering the one question all potential donors ask themselves, "***Why should I give to this organization, instead of some other worthy cause?***" it also talks about ways to boost donor generosity, trumpeting your value proposition, ways to cause less friction when asking someone for their personal information, segmenting your audiences, asking for permission before adding someone to your newsletter list, and the all-important three metrics that spell success: traffic, conversions, and average gift.

Ignite Your Donor Passion, in the greater part, discusses the most popular communication channels: websites, blogs, email, newsletters, appeal letters, brochures, presentations, and face-to-face meetings. Each section breaks down the anatomy of what makes an **AMAZING** email, newsletter, brochure, or face-to-face meeting. From there, it discusses the process for launching each method, as well as how it can be used to inform, educate, engage, inspire, and prompt action. Along the way, many sections outline methods for increasing the size of donor files, boosting traffic and conversions, and enhancing donor generosity. The chapter closes with addressing not settling for "Good Enough" and ends with a list of pros and cons.

Ignite Your Donor Passion concludes with a section titled: "What's Working—What's Not," which addresses ways to think about developing a continuous improvement plan. We should always be striving to improve. Vince Lombardi, Hall of Fame football coach of the Green Bay Packers, once said: "Perfection is not attainable, but if we chase perfection, we can catch excellence."

Ignite Your Donor Passion is written with three audiences in mind: organizations starting, those that have stalled, and those seeking to make their organization even more impactful.

Read On!
John D. Leavy
johndleavy@gmail.com

The Roadmap

Anyone who wants to reach their destination safely and successfully relies on roadmaps. Roadmaps provide a starting point and indicate the distance to our destination. The map's features and terrain represent what we'll encounter along the way. Roadmaps help us determine the preferred route and assist us in navigating unfamiliar territory.

In strengthening the relationship between the organization and its potential supporters and partners, whether through the website, social media, newsletter, or email, there are likely five communication goals an organization needs to achieve. They are designed to inform, educate, engage, inspire, and motivate one to take action. *Ignite Your Donor Passion* helps you understand the ins and outs of becoming proficient in achieving all five key areas.

Chapter ONE: Create AMAZING Donor Passion begins by highlighting the five reasons (inform, educate, engage, inspire, and cause action) one might use to communicate with another, and the thirteen ingredients that will make your donor's passion **AMAZING**. The elements discussed range from speaking impactfully and calling donors to action to writing that relates to the reader and being candidly honest. From there, the discussion turns to promoting your value proposition, minimizing friction, and segmenting your audiences. It concludes by defining the all-important metrics to track traffic, conversions, and average gift value.

Downloadable Resource(s):

✓   Create **AMAZING** Donor Passion Questionnaire

Chapter TWO: Create AMAZING Websites begins by discussing the importance of defining website goals before design or development begins. Websites can inform, educate, offer products or services, or collect donations from donors. After a brief discussion on the anatomy of the website, the chapter transitions to outlining what it takes to develop an **AMAZING** website strategy, as well as ways to build website traffic. From there, the discussion deals with measuring success and what it takes to convert visitors into subscribers and donors. Chapter TWO ends with talking about not settling for "Good Enough"—a brief evaluation on what it takes to develop a strong web presence, and a list of pros and cons.

Chapter THREE: Create AMAZING Blogs identifies blogging as a journaling exercise, only in this case, people are looking over your shoulder at what's being written. First, Chapter FIVE covers the anatomy of an **AMAZING** blog's makeup. It then discusses developing a blogging strategy, followed by ways to measure success. Next, building a blog audience is on deck, followed by how to overcome blogger's block. It ends with sections on not settling for "Good Enough," an evaluation exercise to make sure your blogging efforts pay off and closes with a list of pros and cons to help you decide if blogging is really for you.

Downloadable Resource(s):

- ✓ Blog Promotional Email Example 1
- ✓ Blog Promotional Email Example 2

Chapter FOUR: Create AMAZING Email Messages opens by reviewing the anatomy of an **AMAZING** email message. Next, developing an email strategy and boosting your email open-rate are discussed. Converting recipients into subscribers and donors, and measuring success, are perhaps the most pressing topics in this section. The chapter concludes with segments on not settling for "Good Enough," an evaluation exercise, and a list of pros and cons.

Downloadable Resource(s):

- ✓ Appeal Letter Example
- ✓ Newsletter w/Email Example
- ✓ Blog Promotional Email Example
- ✓ Event Promotional Email Series Example 1
- ✓ Event Promotional Email Series Example 2
- ✓ Event Promotional Email Series Example 3
- ✓ Event Promotional Email Series Example 4

Chapter FIVE: Create AMAZING Newsletters identifies the role a newsletter can play in keeping constituents informed. The publication can be either long or short and can be released weekly or monthly. This chapter first focuses on the anatomy of an **AMAZING** newsletter and then discusses building a newsletter strategy, as well as how measuring success can help produce positive results. From there, it talks about assembling an audience, not settling for "Good Enough," and ends with an evaluation exercise and a list of pros and cons to ensure your publication bears fruit.

Downloadable Resource(s):

✓ Newsletter Example

✓ Newsletter Promotional Email Example

Chapter SIX: Create AMAZING Appeal Letters discusses how newsletters or email blasts are not appeal letters. Appeal letters serve a defined purpose. Chapter SIX starts by outlining the anatomy of an **AMAZING** appeal letter and then showcases the elements of a strong appeal letter strategy. From there, the discussion turns to converting recipients into giving partners and ways to measure success. Not settling for "Good Enough," an evaluation exercise, and the pros and cons close out this portion.

Downloadable Resource(s):

✓ Appeal Letter Example

Chapter SEVEN: Create AMAZING Brochures shows how this form of communication lends credibility and legitimacy to an organization. The publication can feature an organization's projects, as well as its vision, mission, and purpose. They can be printed and mailed to potential donors or sent by email. Brochures need to be professionally done. A solid brochure strategy might include an introductory piece to use when meeting with potential new donors, as well as a supplemental conversation starter to discuss the various projects. Alternatively, the brochure may be used to examine a planned event or an end-of-year fundraising effort. Success may be hard to gauge, so be diligent. This chapter discusses developing a solid brochure strategy, measuring success, and concludes with not settling for "Good Enough" section, an analysis exercise, and a list of pros and cons.

Downloadable Resource(s):

- ✓ AGMT Brochure Example
- ✓ R&S Brochure Example

Chapter EIGHT: Create AMAZING Presentations lists three dynamics of a typical presentation: the slides, the content, and the presenter. This chapter breaks down the essential factors that make each of these ingredients successful. It also discusses building a presentation strategy that yields positive results, along with methods for measuring success. It concludes with not settling for "Good Enough", a way to evaluate the presentation's effectiveness, and ends with a list of pros and cons.

Downloadable Resource(s):

- ✓ Presentation Slides Example
- ✓ Presentation Slides Worksheet

Chapter NINE: Create AMAZING Face-to-face Meetings talks about how successful face-to-face meetings do not happen without planning, preparation, practice, and prayer. They are, by far, the best way to either begin building relationships with potential supporters or to secure new donors. Chapter NINE includes: developing a contact list, putting together a call script, setting appointments, developing a way to keep the face-to-face meetings on track, measuring the results, and finishing with not settling for "Good Enough," an assessment, and a list of pros and cons.

Downloadable Resource(s):

- ✓ Potential Contacts Worksheet
- ✓ Appointment Setting Script Example
- ✓ Appointment Setting Script Worksheet
- ✓ Information Card Example
- ✓ Donor Card Example
- ✓ Face-to-face Meeting Script Example
- ✓ Face-to-face Meeting Script Worksheet

Chapter TEN: Create AMAZING Photos highlights how photos play a significant role in supporting the communication that takes place between the organization and its supporters. Photos corroborate the story being told. They must convey emotion, passion, and reality. Photos tell what's happening on the ground. They draw the reader into the story. They create a connection. This chapter identifies common mistakes organizations make when selecting inappropriate photos for their communication.

Chapter ELEVEN: Create AMAZING Communication Plans begins by identifying thirteen elements that are needed to produce positive results when conversing with constituents. Key ingredients include defining the target audience, developing a sound and compelling message, determining a realistic budget, planning for two-way communication, and monitoring the results. It finishes with a list of pros and cons.

Downloadable Resource(s):

✓ Sample Communication Plan by Donor Schedule
✓ Sample Communication Plan by Channel

Chapter TWELVE: What's Working—What's Not begins by listing some of the most common reasons communication between two entities may fail. Reasons include undefined goals, mission misalignment, lack of clear calls-to-action, and content that was not compelling or did not meet donor-centric standards. From there, it lists areas within each communication mishap that are usually prone to failure. Mishaps include websites not designed by professionals, blogs lacking passion, sending emails without a way to track opens, sending newsletters to recipients who did not opt in, and appeal letters with no stated purpose or appeal.

You'll find loads of Tips, Show & Tell Examples, and worksheets throughout *Ignite Your Donor Passion*.

Tips: The author shares as much information and wisdom as possible in these brief pages. Tips such as "Personalize your email salutation" help people take advantage of what's most successful.

Show & Tell: There are dozens of Examples, Worksheets, and spreadsheets labeled: Show & Tell— the Worksheets are editable, so you'll be able to apply what you've learned instantly. Modify the handouts and use them for your next communication campaign.

ONE

(28 MIN READ)

Create **AMAZING** Donor Passion

Writing to someone needs a purpose. No one should have to wonder, as they begin reading an email, news, or support letter, why they've received the communique. The message, short or long, must have a purpose, and the purpose needs to be evident from the get-go.

After stating the reason for writing, the balance of the copy should support, explain, or expand on the stated reason, and then conclude with a closing thought or a request for action, if that is the goal of communicating with the person.

Inform, Educate, Engage, Inspire, Cause Action

If the purpose is to *inform* potential supporters or donors about what's happening on the ground, be specific. Share as many details as you believe prudent and relevant to the story.

If fundraising has been less than stellar during the past year, be honest with your donors in laying out your current financial situation and where you need to be to continue the work. Give them something precise to pray about or to support.

If the purpose of the message is to **educate** people about raising up local pastors and planting churches in Ghana in the subregion of West Africa, perhaps this might be a good educational angle:

> *First, you need to close the geographic gap that exists between Ghana and the US. The distance between Colorado Springs, Colorado, and Kumasi, Ghana, is approximately 6,638 miles. That's a long way for someone unfamiliar with the region to guess what situations people face every day. Next, people need to understand the work in terms of the needed resources and timing. Please note that there are seven cities you aim to reach over the next three years. Raising up five pastors and planting the first home groups takes six to nine months. Then, highlight the necessary resources and finances required. From there, those who read the email will understand the organization's vision and the amount of hard work ahead of the team.*

In writing emails that **engage**, grab the reader's attention at once. Tell a great story. Write in short sentences. Use active voice. Ask open-ended or thought-provoking questions. Use POWERFUL words that connect with the reader. Write expecting the reader to respond— be prepared to answer the inquiries or comments promptly.

Engagement requires action by both parties. The communication should not flow in only one direction.

Inspiring the reader takes preparation and thought. Words cannot be just thrown down on paper.

Use pictures or photos that show the work in action. Showcase the impact the organization is making.

Use titles and graphics that help convey emotion.

Write as if you're conversing with a best friend.

Know the audience and understand where their passions lie.

If you're still stuck on how to get started, read inspiring communiques by others and learn from those who are having success.

Motivating an individual to *act* is much easier if you clearly state what you expect them to do. It's known as the call to action. Have you seen support or newsletters that have a little-noticed sentence at the very bottom?

The reader is expected to conclude that the organization is in urgent need and now would be the perfect time to support the work—and to support it in a significant way. Has this practice ever been effective for you in giving or asking?

Don't make asking for help or financial support an afterthought. Keep it at the forefront of your message if that's the message's intent. Don't tell a great story and then expect people to draw their own conclusions about supporting the effort.

Don't see asking for money as a necessary evil. Think of it as giving the person an opportunity to be involved in God's work. You're just the messenger, either in making the need known or in representing the person in need who cannot be there to ask in person. Some people give, while others don't. Keep trying.

Writing with impact takes time, patience, and practice. It includes the 13 ingredients talked about in this chapter. The entire list of elements is not used in unison, nor is it necessarily used in this order.

If you're new to writing with impact, consider selecting a term or two from the forthcoming list and incorporating those elements into your writing. Once you have conquered the basics, move on to using a few components until you feel comfortable using all the ingredients mentioned.

Saying It Impactfully

Expressing ideas with impact requires some artful writing. Some of those tools you thought were not very useful during high school English class finally come into play.

Writing impactfully requires the use of action words and action verbs. If you're stuck on what words to use, browse the Internet looking for "positive" or "action" words or verbs—there are hundreds.

Writing impactfully requires the message to be written in *active,* not *passive* voice. Remember, the *active voice* describes a sentence where the subject performs the action stated by the verb. In *passive voice* sentences, the subject is acted upon by the verb.

Bob posted the video on Facebook. (active voice)
The video was posted on Facebook by Bob. (passive voice)

Sell the story with headlines that grab the reader's attention.

Write with emotion.

Make the story sound like it's coming from a human being. Be real. Be authentic.

Convince the reader why they should care. Don't focus on just a few members in the readership audience. Take a broad approach when writing. Try to include as many readers as possible.

Focus on what the audience wants to hear the most. This means the writer must know their audience well. Don't lump everyone into one general, non-descript assemblage.

Adding the "Personal Touch"

Always use the person's first name if you know the person personally, or their first and last name if you're just acquaintances. Forget the "Dear Donor," "Dear Friend," or "Dear Supporter" monikers. What could be more impersonal than not using a person's name when you know you are aware of it?

Did you know?
Personalizing the email can boost the open-rate by **270%**.
(NextAfter.com Experiment #5707)

Using a person's name immediately draws them into the conversation and puts them at ease.

Sign off the same way the message starts. If first names are used in the salutation, end with your first name. This puts both parties on an equal footing.

Calling All Donors to Action

Think of a call to action as a conversion device. Calls to action require a higher level of commitment. These mechanisms also serve to move the potential supporter further along in the decision-making process.

> ### Did you know?
> Increased authority and an active call to action produced a **64%** surge in downstream conversions.
> (NextAfter.com Experiment #7844)

The call to action might ask visitors to subscribe to a free, monthly newsletter or receive a complimentary eBook.

Keep in mind that it is just as essential to have a strategy that addresses what happens after the visitor decides. What happens after they sign up for the free webinar or download the free eBook?

Create urgency in the recipient's mind by giving the call to action an expiration date, real or imaginary.

Do not use motion, a smiling face, a waving hand, or a bouncing arrow in the call to action. It only distracts the visitor.

Delivering a Professional Look and Feel

Remember, when handing a person, a business card or brochure, or sending them an email, newsletter, or speaking out on social media, it needs to instill confidence and trust in the organization.

It's quite likely that one may never personally meet many of the organization's potential supporters. So, the material initially sent out represents the organization's first impression. Here are some thoughts to consider when building the organization's professional look and feel:

- Have a professional design the materials for the organization (logo, business card, brochure, website.) Skip the brother-in-law or neighbor-down-the-street connection. How many of us would opt to go under the knife of the cheapest brain surgeon in town?

Did you know?

According to *web credibility research* from Stanford, **75%** of users admit to making judgements about an organization based on their web design.

- Be sure all the materials have what is called a "family-look." In other words, use the same colors and font styles. The materials, spread out on the table, should appear to have all come from the same organization.

- Make sure to use good photography. Pictures that tell great stories. Images that load fast on the website and mobile devices. Images that are slow to load cause visitors to go elsewhere. Use readable photos, regardless of where they appear. It does little good to show someone a picture the size of a postage stamp.

- Spelling and grammar checking are essential. Find someone to proofread everything before it is published or posted on the web.

- Ensure that the information being conveyed is not only well thought out but also well laid out.

- Always leave some open real estate (white space), whether designing a brochure, newsletter, or web page. Not every square inch needs to be crowded with text and images.

Being Results-Oriented

Donors want to know they've made a wise investment in the organization's work. They want to be reassured that the funds are making the most impact possible.

Publish regular reports on the progress being made and the impact being realized. The reports can be a simple paragraph letting the supporters know all is well—the projects are on time and on budget. Better yet, would be the announcement that things are ahead of schedule and under budget.

Focusing on the Donor, Not the Organization

Avoid using words such as "I," "me," "my," "we," or "us." These words tend to remove the reader from the story. Write with a donor-centric approach. Here's an example:

"We worked hard and now we have built a new dormitory for our girls."

"Because of your generosity and others, the girls can now enjoy their new, 20-bed dormitory."

The first sentence focuses on the organization. The organization was obviously involved. However, the sentence overlooks the donor's contribution. The second sentence outlines what was accomplished because of the donor's support.

Whether sending an email, writing a support letter, or creating a blog post, keep the focus on the donor's involvement. Write as if they are an active part of the team—even if the work is being done thousands of miles away.

Relating to the Reader

Drop the "church-speak" or "ministry mumbo jumbo". Write in plain, simple language that people understand. Using words or expressions that supporters are unfamiliar with makes readers uncomfortable. They may not be on board with the latest terminology or how things are explained in foreign cultures and therefore feel left in the dark.

It's essential to tune the writing to the readership.

It may be advantageous to use specific terms. If that's the case, then bring people along slowly by explaining the use of the words or phrase the first time they appear.

Timing is Everything

Timing has always been and will always mean "everything." End-of-the-year support letters cannot be sent out the last week of December with the expectation that they will be enormously successful. Newsletters cannot be sent out randomly or on a haphazard schedule. Replies on social media need to be almost immediate.

Each organization needs to find the times that work best for its supporters and their team members. If a newsletter is being sent out, do more people read the publication if it's delivered in the morning or the afternoon? Do more readers open the email at the beginning of the month or at the end of the month? Are supporters more involved in social media between 9 AM and 11 AM or between 3 PM and 5 PM? Are the phone calls more successful during the week or on weekends?

Take the time necessary to discover the best times to send out the various materials you use to communicate and engage with your potential supporters and donors.

Staying Consistent

Consistency is closely tied to *"Timing is Everything."* Once the organization determines the best times to communicate and engage their supporters, it's essential to stick with those times. There are, of course, always exceptions that may vary from the schedule. Ensure the reason is apparent to all parties involved.

If the organization has several irons in the fire, such as sending out monthly newsletters along with occasional emails, posting on a blog, and engaging in social media, make sure the timing of all the activities does not overburden the team.

Don't over-commit. Start slowly and gradually increase the pace as success is achieved.

Meeting on Common Ground

Be sensitive enough to understand how people want to engage with the organization. Younger audiences prefer communicating on social media in short bursts. They'll prefer watching a video instead of reading a three-page newsletter. They're on Facebook, Instagram, and Snapchat. The more veteran crowd enjoys reading and wouldn't mind receiving a newsletter by email. Some still prefer receiving their information by US Mail.

Synchronize the communication methods to the preferences of the intended audience.

Closing the Gap

It's 6,638 miles from Colorado Springs, Colorado, to Ghana, West Africa. Ghana experiences dry winters and hot, rainy summers. The monsoon season lasts from May to September. Most of the roads are unpaved, and you won't find a Starbucks at every busy intersection. Things are very different. The people are different. The environment is different. The business sectors are different. The political climate is different.

It's essential to bridge the gap between the donor and the location where the work is being done. Write some pieces that feature the differences between the two geographic areas. Weave bits of information within the stories you tell. Help potential supporters and donors understand and appreciate the breadth and scope of the challenges faced by the people being helped.

Being Blatantly Honest

Don't hide the fact or be embarrassed that the fundraising efforts are behind. Many support letters include, in very small print, sometimes in gray lettering, at the very bottom of the letter, a sentence that resembles this example:

> *To support our ministry, click here. Thank you.*

Organizations must be transparent and honest with their supporters. If the goal is to raise $2,200 a month and one finds oneself $1,500 behind for the month, how will the supporters know or understand the dire situation that exists?

If the goal of the newsletter, email campaign, or support letter is to raise support, then the readers must know the purpose of the communiques.

Whether the funds are being used for personal support or are being raised for an upcoming project, it's essential to keep donors informed early.

If the process has been difficult and you feel uncomfortable with the fundraising efforts, please let the people supporting them know. Allow them to share any wisdom they may have. Ask them to lift your situation up in prayer.

Expressing Urgency

It's not smart to cry wolf when sending out each monthly support letter. However, supporters need to be aware of pending emergencies that could jeopardize the work.

Let donors know regularly how things are progressing, whether the need is spiritual, financial, emotional, or related to some construction schedule that has fallen behind. No one deals well with surprises. Donors are surely interested in all aspects of the work but certainly care most about those doing the labor.

Create a schedule to keep donors informed. Perhaps spiritual requests can go out monthly, but also when a dire situation arises. The balance of the information could be included in a scheduled newsletter that is sent out regularly.

Whatever the plan, stick to the schedule and minimize surprises.

Boosting Donor Generosity

There are various ways to increase donor generosity. More than a dozen is listed here. You'll need to review the options and select the ones that you believe work best for the organization. Here's a sampling of what turns up if you ask other non-profits:

- Give your donors bragging rights. Consistently let your supporters know that their generosity is the reason the work is progressing so well.

- Regularly ask your donors for support. Forget the one, awkwardly written the week before Christmas.

- Inform your donors about the various giving options the organization offers.

- Let donors know that organizations run smoothly when they're able to budget expenses. Encourage your supporters to give through monthly electronic payments (ACH).

- This may be a no-brainer but make giving to the organization as easy as possible. Remove any impediments from the payment process.

- Consider hosting a special giving day, such as Giving Tuesday (the Tuesday after Thanksgiving).

> **Did you know?**
> Whole Whale is predicting **$201 million** will be raised this #GivingTuesday a **20%** increase over last year's **$160 million**.

- Ensure that donors understand the scope and scale of your vision, not just for this year, but for years to come.

- Don't assume people know how to be biblical stewards. Perhaps sending them a study on the subject would be helpful.

- Always discuss the impact the work is having and how people's lives are being changed.

- Keep your most committed donors well-informed.

- Tell stories that tap into people's empathy.

- Ask them to volunteer (time), ask for their advice or ideas.

- Let your supporters know about your successes and the impact the work is having on people's lives. Share solid results. Donors want to trust that their funds are being used wisely.

- Focus on the "why" more and less on the "what" and "how." For example, it's beneficial for people to know that the new dormitory is opening next month and that 30 new beds are available. It's good for them to know it's a cinderblock building with a metal roof with five windows per side. It's also good to know that a sponsor family will be housed with the children. But keep the focus on how the children's lives are changed because of the new dormitory. The children will be well cared for, safer, and in a cleaner environment, looked after by a loving couple. They'll be happier. Highlight what the children are learning because they are under the watchful eye of caring, Christian caregivers.

Trumpeting Your Value Proposition

An organization's value proposition, or uniqueness, should be obvious, concise, understandable, and evident in all its communications. Don't be too proud to shout it from the rooftops.

It answers the one question on every potential donor's mind, *"**Why should I give to this organization instead of some other worthy cause?**"*

Kissmetrics.com has a sound definition for Value Proposition: A believable collection of the most persuasive reasons people should notice you and take the action you're asking."

Here are a few you might be familiar with:

Walmart – Save Money Live Better

Apple – The Experience IS the Product

Uber – The Smartest Way to Get Around

Young Life – You Were Made for This

Navigators – Disciples Making Disciples

1Man2Another – Helping Men Navigate Life

Causing Less Friction

People make numerous minor decisions before they make a major one. Think about the thought process one goes through when receiving an email.

- The message hits the inbox, and your MacBook chirps its arrival.
- You glance at the Sender's name.
- Decide if you have the time to look further.
- Maybe the Subject line interests you, perhaps not.
- You open the message.
- Now you quickly read the first half sentence or so.
- Again, you decide whether to proceed or not.
- You decide you have a moment and read on.
- Halfway through the email, you conclude it's not urgent and does not require a quick reply.

- It's back to work.

Did you know?
A radical redesign that reduces friction and increases the force of the value proposition affects donor conversion by **134%**. (NextAfter.com Experiment #5729)

Consider how this process is magnified when you decide to click on the link within the email and navigate to the donation page. Most of the initial ten decisions are made once again. And if you do decide to give a gift to the organization, there are all those personal banking questions one must consider before hitting the 'DONATE' button.

A person might make dozens of minor decisions before deciding to give $25 to an organization.

Each decision causes some level of friction. The more friction there is, the greater the chance the person will leave the donation process before hitting the 'DONATE' button.

Gain   Pain

Friction Meter

What's causing the friction is the struggle between *value* and *cost*? Does what the person is being asked to do cost them more than the perceived value of what they'll gain?

Consider asking a person for their email address and offering them nothing in return. The person is asked to give up their email address (value) for nothing in exchange (cost). The friction here is intolerable. Few, if any, people would give their email address to an organization without receiving something in return.

Here's another example. Think of asking a person for their postal address, phone number, and email address as opposed to just asking for their email. The friction generated by asking for all three pieces of personal information is huge.

People can only assume that if they give someone their phone number, they'll start receiving calls—unsolicited, unwanted, unwelcome calls during dinner hour. If an organization provides its postal address, is it reasonable for them to assume they will shortly be receiving junk mail?

It cannot be overstated that the email sent, the donation page people are routed to, and the donation form itself, which captures a person's information, must be finely tuned. Free of any distractions. Free of any unnecessary hoops people should jump through. The donation form should only request the necessary information to process the gift, without collecting any additional details.

Making the gifting process more difficult than it needs to be only builds friction—and friction leads to rejection.

Ensure the value exceeds the cost.

Segmenting Your Audience

Once the mechanisms are in place to collect email addresses, the next task is to divide the audience into what are called *personas*.

Per•son•a – the aspect of someone's character that is presented to or perceived by others.

Let's consider assigning *personas* to volunteers, team or board members, potential donors, and regular donors. You may also want to categorize donors into groups such as one-time givers, monthly donors, and major donors.

We'll want to assign *personas* to our donor file because one size does not fit all. It's important to send out personalized, meaningful messages to each group.

Some supporters give regularly, others monthly, and still others when a crisis arises. Certain people give more than others. Some individuals want to know more about what's happening in detail. Some individuals want to be more engaged than others. Some may offer to volunteer, others won't. Some are interested in spiritual well-being, while others may be attentive to construction or environmental projects. Some want to hear from you regularly, while others may think hearing from you every month or so is sufficient.

To achieve the right balance when sending out email messages with the right topics to the correct audience, the overall group needs to be segmented. The sender also needs to be tuned into each donor's passion.

There are times when only current donors need to receive the message. There are times when potential givers need to be educated and encouraged to join the cause.

The delineation between *personas* can be simple or complex. If the system is designed to achieve the goal of sending the right message to the right group, at the right time, and in the right way, then all's fine.

Asking for Permission—Don't Assume

Seth Godin wrote a notable book in 1999 titled "*Permission Marketing*." In fact, he coined the phrase "permission marketing." Seth's point is that it makes more sense to ask someone's permission to send them something rather than filling their inbox with unwanted material or interrupting their day.

We might say that permission marketing is asking our potential readers to opt-in or subscribe to our newsletter before assuming they want to be added to our circulation database.

People who don't ask readers to "opt-in" may be afraid of the truth. They don't want to know that only 13% of the email addresses they are sending to are valid or belong to people who care about what is being received.

Isn't it logical to talk to the people who want to hear from you or read what you have to say? If only 13% of donors want to listen to the message, then focus on those individuals alone. The person who does not want to hear from an organization is far less likely to become an avid supporter.

Traffic, Conversions, and Average Gift

Traffic, *Conversions*, and *Average Gift* are the actual measurements of success that need to be tracked in any engagement campaign.

In a simple example, think of *traffic* and the number of website visitors or the number of people who receive a support letter. *Conversions* would be the number of people who download an eBook or subscribe to a newsletter. They've taken some action. *The average gift is* the average donation amount generated per donor during a campaign. If 25 people gave $5,000 to a cause, the average gift would be $200.

Whether the communication vehicle is a newsletter, social media, an email campaign, or a support letter, it's vital to know the *traffic*, *conversion*, and *average gift* numbers to judge if the effort being expended is producing positive results.

> **Did you know?**
> Leaving a donation recommendation off the form saw
> a **276%** increase.
> (NextAfter.com Experiment #6473)

Here's a series of questions that can help uncover areas where communication might be lacking or not as strong as it could or should be to be effective.

 **Find the Create AMAZING Donor Passion Questionnaire at the end of this chapter.**

Consider answering these questions yourself and have either your advisory team or a few trusted supporters complete the same exercise to gain as much insight as possible.

Create AMAZING Donor Passion Questionnaire

Answer the following questions on a scale of 1 to 5 (with 1 representing Weak and 5 standing for Very Strong.)

If any item is rated 2 or less then attention is needed in this area to make this communication piece as efficient and effective as possible.

Be honest.

1. **Inform, Educate, Engage, Inspire, Cause Action**
   (Rate these five separately.)

   How satisfied are you with...**Informing**? _____

   How satisfied are you with...**Educating**? _____

   How satisfied are you with...**Engaging**? _____

   How satisfied are you with...**Inspiring**? _____

   How satisfied are you with...**Causing Action**? _____

2. How satisfied are you with...**Saying it Impactfully?**

   _____

3. How satisfied are you with...**Adding the "Personal Touch?"**

   _____

4. How satisfied are you with...**Calling All Donors to Action?**

   _____

5. How satisfied are you with...**Look and feel?**

   _____

6. How satisfied are you with...**Being Results Oriented?**

    _____

7. How satisfied are you with...**Focusing on the Donor, Not the Organization?**

    _____

8. How satisfied are you with...**Relating to the Reader?**

    _____

9. How satisfied are you with...**Timing is Everything?**

10. How satisfied are you with...**Staying Consistent?**

    _____

11. How satisfied are you with...**Meeting on Common Ground?**

    _____

12. How satisfied are you with...**Closing the Gap?**

    _____

13. How satisfied are you with...**Being Blatantly Honest?**

    _____

14. How satisfied are you with...**Expressing Urgency?**

    _____

15. How satisfied are you with...**Boosting Donor Generosity?**

     _____

16. How satisfied are you with...**Trumpeting Your Value Proposition?**

     _____

17. How satisfied are you with...**Causing Less Friction?**

     _____

18. How satisfied are you with...**Segmenting Your Audience?**

     _____

19. How satisfied are you with...**Asking for Permission – Don't Assume?**

     _____

20. **Traffic, Conversions, and Average Gift**

    (Rate these three separately.)

    How satisfied are you with...**Traffic**? _____
    How satisfied are you with...**Conversions**? _____
    How satisfied are you with...**Average Gift**? _____

SHOW & TELL

Create AMAZING Donor Passion Questionnaire (1)

Create AMAZING Donor Passion Questionnaire

Answer the following questions on a scale of 1 to 5 (with 1 representing Weak and 5 standing for Very Strong.)

If any item is rated 2 or less then attention is needed in this area to make this communication piece as efficient as possible.

Be honest.

1. **Inform, Educate, Engage, Inspire, Cause Action**

(Rate these five separately.)

How satisfied are you with...**Informing?** _____

How satisfied are you with...**Educating?** _____

How satisfied are you with...**Engaging?** _____

How satisfied are you with...**Inspiring?** _____

How satisfied are you with...**Causing Action?** _____

2. How satisfied are you with...**Saying it Impactfully?** _____
3. How satisfied are you with...**Adding the "Personal Touch?"** _____
4. How satisfied are you with...**Calling All Donors to Action?** _____
5. How satisfied are you with...**Delivering a Professional Look-and-fe** _____
6. How satisfied are you with...**Being Results Oriented?** _____
7. How satisfied are you with...**Focusing on the Donor Not the Organ** _____

Copyright © 2018 Project Caleb

---

8. How satisfied are you with...**Relating to the Reader?** _____
9. How satisfied are you with...**Timing is Everything?** _____
10. How satisfied are you with...**Staying Consistent?** _____
11. How satisfied are you with...**Meeting on Common Ground?** _____
12. How satisfied are you with...**Closing the Gap?** _____
13. How satisfied are you with...**Being Blatantly Honest?** _____
14. How satisfied are you with...**Expressing Urgency?** _____
15. How satisfied are you with...**Boosting Donor Generosity?** _____
16. How satisfied are you with...**Trumpeting Your Value Proposition?** _____
17. How satisfied are you with...**Causing Less Friction?** _____
18. How satisfied are you with...**Segmenting Your Audience?** _____
19. How satisfied are you with...**Asking for Permission-Don't Assume?** _____
20. Traffic, Conversions, and Average Gift

(Rate these three separately.)

How satisfied are you with...**Traffic?** _____

How satisfied are you with...**Conversions?** _____

How satisfied are you with...**Average Gift?** _____

Copyright © 2018 Project Caleb

Download at:

johndleavy.com/PC/CreateAMAZINGDonorPassionQ.pdf

TWO

(19 MIN READ)

Create **AMAZING**
Websites

T he website must have a professional look and feel. The menu navigation should be intuitive and easy to pilot. There needs to be compelling content that is well thought-out with obvious calls to action. Treating every website visitor the same is a crucial mistake too often made. When potential supporters, donors, and volunteers visit the site, have a method to route each group promptly to their expected destinations.

Websites perform a variety of functions for an organization. The website may be where people can donate to the cause or track the progress of a specific project. The site may serve

> "**It's not about the organization even though they own the website.** It's all about the visitor and his or her perceived need or want."

to inform and educate potential supporters, helping them move closer to a decision to contribute. It might house the blog posts. Or its duty might be to serve as a clearinghouse for the organization's downloadable resources and videos.

Anatomy of an **AMAZING** Website

Here's the website (SaveTheStorks.com) of an organization that offers free ultrasounds to expectant mothers

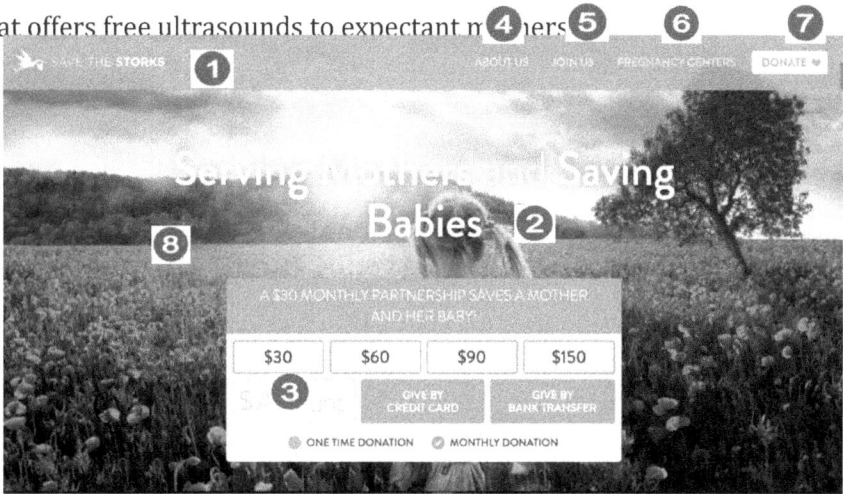

break down's breakdown the page layout:

1. **Logo** – The logo provides visitors with a standard way of getting back to the homepage. Ensure the logo colors are easy on the eyes and that the logo image and text are readable.

2. **Mission Statement** – Their mission—Serving Mothers and Saving Babies is brief, noticeable, and memorable.

3. **Donation Window** – Giving to the organization is simple.

Those who want to give gifts have several choices of amounts and methods.

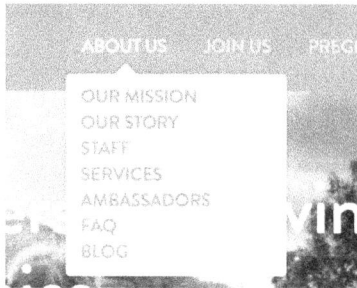

4. **About Us** – Visitors can learn more about the organization's efforts by selecting the "About Us" button. The menu selections feature pull-down menus, allowing visitors to navigate to the desired information on the site quickly.

5. **Join Us** – Visitors are welcome to join the cause.

6. **Pregnancy Centers** – Allows visitors to understand why going mobile makes sense. They can also find out about the stork bus features and their locations across the United States.

7. **Donate Button** – A Donate button is also available on the main menu bar. As visitors navigate the site, they will always be able to see how to be involved financially.

> **Did you know?**
> Visually emphasizing the Donate button boosted the
> conversion rate by **189%**.
> (NextAfter.com Experiment #1698)

8. **Background Image** – Don't miss the "hero" image used as a background.

Developing a Website Strategy

A website may be the first impression an organization leaves with a visitor. With billions of websites competing for a visitor's attention, the chances that an organization is given a second look are slim.

*"**Don't make too many alterations to the website content at one time.** It will be difficult to determine which message is working best."*

First impressions are everything. Make sure the web design is not committing these all too familiar mistakes:

- **The website only has eight seconds to grab the visitor's attention** – as faster computers serve websites quickly, the visitor's attention span shrinks. This means that organizations have less and less time to capture the attention of their visitors. Your message should be concise, relevant, and timely.

- **Does the web design create an atmosphere of trust and confidence**? Websites that resemble dark alleys do very little to calm the visitor's worries. Potential supporters are unlikely to share their personal or financial information with someone they do not trust. The website needs to look credible, professional, and secure.

- **Does the website keep visitors coming back?** – Relevant, fresh content keeps people coming back to a website. People need a reason to revisit. This is a significant reason blogging is so successful. Blogging about what's happening and what is on the near horizon leads to a larger readership.

- **Does the website design effectively persuade visitors to act?** – Calls to action need to be obvious, timely, attractive, and compelling. There's nothing wrong with having several calls to action (text links or images) on a single web page. Some website visitors react to a paragraph of text, while an image or picture may stimulate more visitors. Try both.

Did you know?
Adding a specific campaign slide-down to the homepage increased the conversion rate by **474%**.
(NextAfter.com Experiment #7772)

- **Don't treat every website visitor the same** – Think about a trip to the zoo. Everyone who enters the front gate receives a map, and each family member wants to head off in a different direction to see their favorite animal, whether it be lions, tigers, or bears. Letting people browse only leads to lost opportunities. Create a website with decision-making paths that guide visitors to the information they need. Think of the main reasons visitors come to the website and create a special spot for each of their needs on the homepage. From the website homepage, create paths that each visitor group can follow. Once they have the necessary information, they'll be ready to make their decision.

Here are a series of questions to consider when deciding to launch a website for the organization:

> **Did you know?**
> Addressing a new segment of donors on the homepage can impact donor conversion by **46%**.
> (NextAfter.com Experiment #6446)

What's the website's purpose? – The site may have a single purpose or multiple reasons to exist: to inform and educate, to acquire new email addresses, to generate gifts, assemble volunteers, or to make products or services available. Ensure that visitors to the site immediately understand why the site exists and how they can learn more about what interests them the most.

Have the website's audiences been defined? – The site may serve a single audience, or its objective may be to serve multiple groups. Define the website's goals before development begins. If the site will serve potential supporters, donors, and volunteers, ensure that the group can quickly gain access to the information and resources they need.

What resources and information will the site hold? – Websites typically house all sorts of information and resources. There might be eBooks for free or for sale. There may be videos to watch or resources to download. There may be special offers, gifts, or discounts available. There may be blog posts or newsletters.

How will the website be promoted? – With billions of websites already on the Internet and more being developed every day, visitors won't automatically start showing up at the front door of a new website. Promote the site by mentioning it in appeals and newsletters. Place links on social platforms that direct users back to the website. Have a website link at the bottom of your email signature. Prominently display the website name in all literature distributed to constituents and potential donors.

Who manages the site? – The website cannot manage itself. It needs looking after. Someone needs to be responsible for keeping the software, information, and resources up to date. Files may become inaccessible, and links may become broken. A person should review the site to ensure everything is working correctly. Try to download all the resources and test them to ensure everything is in working order.

What about a maintenance schedule? – Information on the website becomes obsolete or out of date. Review the site material on a regular schedule, such as quarterly, to ensure all information and resources are still current and accessible.

Building Your Website Traffic

There are costly ways to increase website traffic, and then there are less expensive ways to acquire new website visitors. Some larger, more well-established organizations rely on Google Pay-per-click campaigns, Facebook Ads, and Search Engine Optimization (SEO) to attract new audience members.

There are other, less expensive, methods of attracting new visitors to the website—let's concentrate on those.

- **Get Social** – If the organization uses social media, then encourage cross-platform visits. Post content on Facebook, then urge the Facebook members to visit the website.

- **Write Irresistible Headlines** – Irresistible headlines catch people's attention. Headlines make or break a great story. Don't neglect the headline when writing the story.

- **Write Compelling Accounts** – People enjoy being encouraged, inspired, and excited. Write with passion. Tell first-rate stories, don't wander, and strive to keep things brief. Include real details and great photos. Tap into the reader's emotions and find ways to place the reader in the narrative. It's always a bonus to the story when the recipients being ministered to can be brought into the account.

- **Invite Others to Guest Blog** – Contact organizations that are working in the exact location. Build a rapport with influencers and trade blog posts for mutual benefits.

- **Post Content on LinkedIn** – LinkedIn can be a valuable source of connections, despite its association with business and commerce. Join LinkedIn groups that have members interested in the organization's efforts.

- **Interview Leaders in Your Non-profit Space** – Build relationships with influencers in your non-profit space. Share thoughts and see if there exist opportunities for collaborative endeavors.

- **Ensure the Site Is Mobile-Friendly** – The website must be optimized for mobile devices.

Did you know?

By 2018 the number of mobile users checking their email is expected to rise to **80%**.

- **Reply if People Comment** – Be prompt when replying to people who comment on blog posts and social media. If people think you're interested, they'll be interested.

- **Incorporate Videos** – With most of the people in the world carrying smartphones, there's little excuse not to capture videos of the work being done on the ground. Take 2 or 3-minute videos that convey the passion and spirit of the organization's work.

- **Look Around to See What Others Are Doing** – The Internet is a great place to incubate new ideas. Take the time to examine organizations doing similar work and observe how they organize their websites.

- **Blog, Blog, Blog** – The following statistic says it all.

Did you know?

Bloggers that post daily get **5X** more traffic.

Measuring Success

Measuring the success of the website cannot be left to gut

feelings. There are free instruments that can give one the real story of what's happening.

There is a popular WordPress app called All in ONE SEO. It looks like this when running:

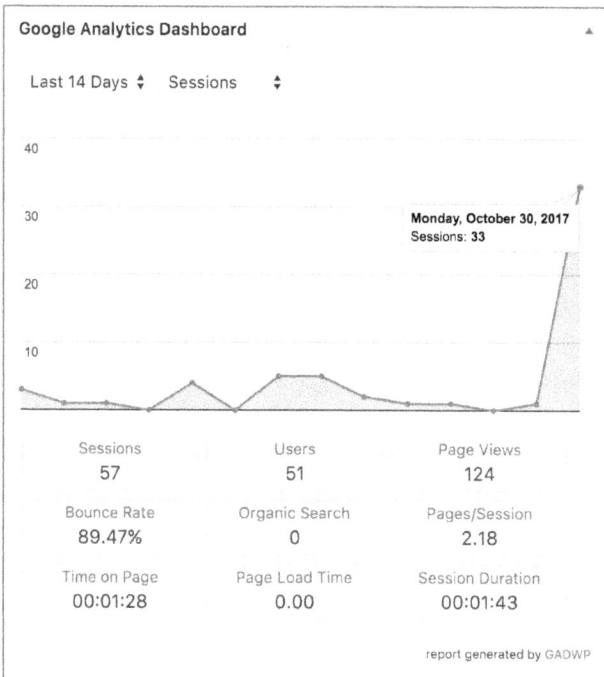

We can see there were 33 Sessions (users or visits) on October 30th. The numbers in the boxes below the graph are the totals for the past 14 days.

Google Analytics is another free tool an organization can use to track user activity. A person can find out how many people visited the website in each timeframe, how long they stayed, where they came from, what webpage they landed on, and from what page they left the site, if and when they decide to return—plus much more.

Here's a snapshot of the Google dashboard:

The strategy here will be to align the website goals and the metrics to track. If the goal of the site is to acquire new email addresses, then we'll want to total the number of people who leave their email address at the site when subscribing or downloading resources. If the goal of the site is to generate new donors, then we'll want to total the gifts given. If the goal of the website is to inform and engage the constituents, are conversations and action taking place?

If the goals are measurable, tracking instruments need to be employed to measure success.

Converting Visitors into Subscribers and Donors

Let's say one of the website's goals is to get visitors to subscribe to the organization's newsletter. With that objective in mind, a strategy needs to be employed.

- First, the newsletter needs to deliver value. It must be full of stories that are compelling, relevant, timely, interesting, donor-centric, and emotionally charged.

- Next, an offer needs to be made available. Suppose a free eBook is offered to those who subscribe to the newsletter?

- Even if the eBook is downloaded, education and nurturing need to take place over a period. Most people arriving at a website are not ready to decide to join, subscribe, or donate.

- The last step in our strategy is to create a follow-up plan. Staying in touch and addressing any questions that arise helps visitors make informed decisions about their giving.

- A plan to acquire new donors is similar. The steps in this plan might look like this:

1. First, gather as much information as possible about the potential donor. What is it that they are passionate about? What do they want to see accomplished?

2. Next, make sure every piece of material sent their way creates a positive experience.

3. Then, describe how the organization is addressing the problem. How are lives being changed? How are the funds being spent?

4. Create a follow-up to ensure every question gets answered thoroughly.

5. Last, make the "ask." Provide potential supporters with options so they can clearly see how they might participate.

Did you know?

Increasing the specificity and conversational tone of the ask increased donations and revenue by **354%**.
(NextAfter.com Experiment #7617)

Don't put the cart before the horse. Build the relationship first. Then attend to any questions that need answering. And, finally, ask the person if they would consider being a part of the effort.

Settling for "Good Enough"

Are the website's objectives being met? If the goal is to inform and educate constituents—are they becoming well-informed? If the goal is to acquire new email addresses—how's that working for you? If the goal is to generate gifts—are donations coming in? Is the visitor traffic building?

Websites make demands on your time, energy, and resources. Make sure the site is paying dividends.

Following is an evaluation exercise to assess the site's usefulness:

Overall

- Does the site offer information and resources not available elsewhere?
- Are analytics (Google Analytics) being run to track visitors on the site?

- Are there defined website goals and are they written down? Are the goals attainable, reasonable, and measurable?

- Is the site-design crisp, well-organized, easy to read, and void of grammatical errors and spelling mistakes?

- Is a maintenance plan in effect to ensure the information on the website is accurate, timely, and relevant?

Audience

- Is the site-design audience-appropriate?

- Are the varied audiences treated differently?

- Are there different resource-types based on audience preference?

Format

- Can the visitor quickly find the information that interests them most?

- Are there "attention-grabbing" headlines and obvious calls-to-action?

- Is the format intuitive when one is looking for information?

- Does the website architecture comply with acceptable industry standards? Is the site vulnerable?

Content

- Does the information convey passion and excitement? Is it timely, relevant, interesting, and donor-centric?

- Does the depth of content match the varied audience needs?

- Are there links within the text to provide resources that go beyond what's covered?

- Is the content free from spelling, grammatical, and other typographical errors?

Engagement

- Is the donation process secure?

- Are visitors engaging?

- Are photos being used to build visual interest?

- Are facts being backed up with authority?

- Are people being asked to act?

Reach

- Can the visitor easily share content from the site?

- Are social links included when appropriate?

- Are links provided for readers to gain more insight into the subject being discussed?

- Are influencers asked to comment?

- Is the content being promoted across social platforms?

- Are there syndication opportunities?

The Pros and Cons

It's always good to consider the options before taking on a new assignment. Here are a set of pros and cons to look over:

Pros and Cons of Websites	
Pros	**Cons**
• Open 24/7 • Credibility • Information exchange • Customer service • Expands reach • Builds engagement • Creates opportunity • Results can be measured	• Requires attention • Information mostly static • May lack individuality • Difficulty reaching the right audience • Cost effective conversions • Slow startup • Could strain the budget

THREE

Create **AMAZING** Blogs

T hink of blogging much like journaling. The only real difference is that people will be looking over your shoulder to see what's written.

> **Did you know?**
> Bloggers that post daily get **5X** more traffic.

Websites convey a button-down, formal, strait-laced, and forward-looking posture for the organization. The information on the web pages is static and rarely changes. Blogging plays a more casual, "this is what the organization is thinking," "what are your thoughts" stance. The website only provides a one-way communication channel. The blog provides a second channel of interaction that draws the reader into the conversation. People can read the blog postings and make their comments. They can also read what others have written.

Blogs provide a great communication link. Take the time to study its components, consider what makes a blog **AMAZING**, and then think about how a blog might be used strategically within your organization.

Anatomy of an **AMAZING** Blog

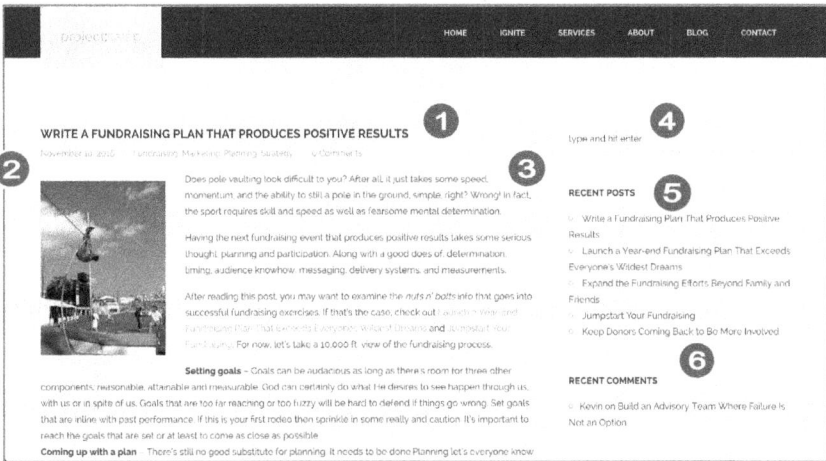

Most blogs have similar formats and options, including:

1. **Title** – Don't pick a title for the post without giving it much thought. It needs to grab the reader's interest. It could be the most important sentence you construct for the post. Titles act to draw the reader into the narrative.

2. **Housekeeping Line** – There's usually a line below the post title that indicates when the post was published, the categories assigned, and the number of comments. These elements can be enabled or disabled.

3. **The Copy** – As to the blog content, you decide on the length. You may want to write longer posts when tackling certain subjects and shorter ones when telling a continuous story. The copy could be informative, educational, inspirational, or prompt the reader to act.

4. **Search Box** – There's frequently a search box in the upper right corner of the page to seek posts based on a word search or phrase.

5. **Recent Posts** – This area shows the most recent posts.

6. **Comments** – This section lists the more recent comments readers made. Some blogs allow comments, others don't.

Archive and Category – *Blogs also contain Archive and Category sections, which are not shown in this illustration.*

Developing a Blogging Strategy

Blogs serve several purposes: they can inform, educate, engage, inspire, or prompt action—they can do all five. The blog could serve as a repository for newsletters, promoting social issues, or raising about catastrophic life-threatening situations around the

Did you know?
80% of all daily traffic to a blog consists of new visitors.

world. It could serve as an information-sharing vehicle or a great way to stay connected with potential supporters and donors.

Blogging builds community and consensus.

Try blogging in an open, modest manner instead of a declarative, "I already know all the answers" format. Blogging should not be a one-way communication channel. Make sure the posts are reader-centric. Try ending posts with open-ended, thought-provoking questions.

The best way to build a solid blog following is to always look for ways to engage the readership. Try a survey occasionally or run an opinion poll from time to time.

Here are a series of questions to consider when developing your blog strategy:

What is the purpose of blogging? – You need to clearly articulate the purpose for the blog. Is it to tell stories about what's happening on the ground where the work is being done? Is it to encourage community between the supporters and the organization? Is it to acquire the email addresses of potential donors? You might be saying yes to all three questions. If that's the case, you'll need a different strategy for each goal. Readers will not conclude that they need to hand over their email address and immediately start supporting the cause just because you're telling them a good story. They'll need to be told what to do.

> **"Don't use the blog to say the same thing over again.** Blogs are supposed to be places where people can read fresh material that does not appear elsewhere."

Who are you writing to? – It's important to identify the audience the blog is directed towards. If the posts are targeting potential supporters, they should inform and educate the readers. If donors are the ideal audience, then the articles need to drill deeper into the details of what's happening on the ground and how the finances are being expended. Donors want to know what's being done is impacting lives.

What are others in your non-profit space saying? – Are you writing about what others have already said? Are there any conflicts you should be aware of? What makes your organization unique?

What keywords will you infuse in your writing? – The search engines scan the blog posts and index them based on certain keywords. If the article is about "orphans in the Congo," make sure to include key phrases that showcase that subject matter.

Will the blog content be syndicated? – Will the content appear as guest posts on other blogs? This is a great way to attract readers from other blogs that may not know about your organization.

How will the blog be promoted? – After publishing each post, think about sending out an email with just the first paragraph and a link back to the post to your supporters and donors. This action causes people to visit your blog more often. Once a month, send out an email recapping what's been posted. Use this strategy to inform people that they can catch up on what's been posted at their convenience.

SHOW & TELL **Find two Blog Promotional Email Examples at the end of this chapter.**

Who will manage the blog? – The blog won't run itself. Someone needs to be responsible. Who will track if the posts are being viewed? Who will verify that the writing is yielding positive results and the goals are being met?

What will be the blogging schedule? – People are in the habit of checking their favorite news sites on a regular basis. They expect their printed magazines to arrive in their mailboxes at the same time each month. Predictability builds expectation. Publish your posts on the same day and time.

Measuring Success

Now that the blogging strategies are set, the success of the efforts needs to be measured. If the goal of the blog is to inform and educate potential supporters and donors, are they visiting the blog and reading the posts? If the goal is to engage the readership, are they commenting on what's being posted? Are they being inspired to join the cause? If you're trying to get people to act, are they leaving their email addresses or visiting the donation page? Are they giving a gift?

Google Analytics can be added to most industry-standard blogs. There are more metrics than need to be discussed here. Let's keep things simple and focus on the numbers that matter most. Metrics such as: *How many people are visiting the blog? Where are they coming from, and how long will they be staying? Is there any interaction? Are people just landing and leaving?*

Metrics tell the story of the blog's success. It's good that people visit the blog. But if the goal is to get people to engage, then they must take some action. Engagement is not a one-way street.

If the blog strategies are not yielding results, adjust them accordingly. If that does not work, then consider diverting your efforts elsewhere.

Did you know?
Blog posts with images get **94%** more views.

Building an Audience

You'll have to work at building a blog readership. People won't start coming by to read what you write just because your blog is on the web. You'll need to employ certain strategies to gain acceptance and build an audience.

- **Collect Subscribers** – Invite people to read your blog by putting a link at the bottom of your email signature. Feature some of the more interesting subjects you're blogging about on your website. Never miss an opportunity to write about what people are talking about most. The news must be relevant, timely, interesting, and packed with helpful information.

- **Syndicate Your Stuff** – The web provides many avenues to syndicate your writings. Use social book marketing to let the larger non-profit communities know what you're writing about.

- **Create Cross Traffic** – Create cross traffic between your social pages, blog, and website by providing links between each platform. That way, the people listening to you on Twitter or Facebook will visit your blog. Tie all your platforms together using text links or images making easy for people to click on interesting items or news stories and move between them.

- **Do Some Guest Appearances** – See if you can trade posts with some influential bloggers in your non-profit space. You write a few posts on her blog, and she writes a few on yours. You'll get exposed to a new audience and perhaps acquire some new readers.

Did you know?
94% of people who share posts do so because they think it might be helpful to others.

- **Walk the Talk** – Most blogs fail because people do not count the cost before launching the experiment. Blogs take time and resources. Ensure you have an ample supply of both and then add a good dose of consistency.

- **Be Interesting** – This goes without saying. Still, unfortunately it needs saying: You're writing must be interesting, motivating, appealing, and cause people to want to act or join in on the discussion. Good bloggers write with passion, conviction, creativity, and perspiration.

- **Calls to action** – Calls to action need to be clear, concise, and obvious. You need to help people through the decision-making process.

- **Examine the Post's Effectiveness** – You could look to see which posts attract the most attention. Those are the subjects the readership is most interested in hearing about. In that case, the solution is simple: write more articles dealing with those subjects.

- **Expand Your Writing –** Check if the content can be refined. If you're not using photos, add some hero images. Include supplemental information so the reader can dig deeper.

- **Get the Readers Involved –** Ask for the reader's opinion. People like to think they're part of the solution.

- **Write Search Engine Friendly –** Pick a few keywords and use them in the headline and throughout the article. Keywords also help sharpen the article's focus.

Battling Blogger's Block

Writers suffer from "writer's block." It's a natural part of the creative process. NASCAR drivers stop winning. Baseball players stop hitting. Football running backs stop scoring touchdowns. Painters have creative lulls. Writer's block is not uncommon. It's not fatal, and there are cures.

So, what is the blogger to do when they run out of subjects to blog about?

- **Change Your Surroundings** – If you've been writing in your home office, try sitting at Starbucks, the city park, by a mountain stream, in the library, or some other location that will stimulate your creative juices. The place could have a fair deal of commotion or be as quiet as the local cemetery. You determine the acceptable noise level.

- **Record Your Writing Ideas** – While you're blogging, talking to people, and doing your own reading or research, ideas will flood your mind. Remember to write them down. They'll be a great resource as time passes.

- **Reschedule to Lessen Stress** – It's difficult to schedule creativity. If you've been setting aside Mondays to blog, try a different day and time. Or if you have been posting once a week, try writing all the posts for a month (when creativity hits) and then schedule them to appear on the blog weekly.

- **Free Write** – Write about anything else that's enjoyable to see if the diversion unlocks the logjam.

- **Read Other Bloggers** – We're not encouraging plagiarism. Reading what others write about can unlock ideas in the writer's mind.

- **Ask Your Readership** – Your readership is a great source of writing ideas. Why not write about what interests' people most? You could ask for their feedback or do a brief survey.

- **Take a Break** – There may come a time when your writing batteries need charging. If you're forcing yourself to write each week, step back from the process for a short time. Spend time doing research and hold off on writing.

- **Write from a Different Perspective** – It may be challenging to look at an issue from a different perspective but give it a try. You may learn more about the problem or yourself.

- **Write Various Length Posts** – If your posts are typically 500 words or more, perhaps writing shorter posts of a few hundred words might be better. Shorter posts can be easier to produce.

- **Read Your Own Archives** – Over time, existing articles may need to be reworked because things have changed. Look over the posts that received the most views and see if there's room for more insight.

- **Troll Social Media for Ideas** – Social platforms like Facebook, Instagram, and others, are loaded with chatter. Scan the platforms for ideas. Be aware of what people are discussing. You can add to the conversations and then draw people back to your blog for more details.

- **Browse the Non-profit Sites** – The non-profit association sites are loaded with good articles and ideas. Pay attention to what people are seeking. See if you can add the desired information back to your blog.

- **Peruse the Internet** – There are plenty of ideas on how to break writer's block. Here's one: When searching the web, this idea came up to include holidays or special events when blogging:

It doesn't take much imagination to incorporate holidays such as Memorial Day, the Fourth of July, or Labor Day into your writing. How about the National Whatever Days you hear about and wonder what was that group thinking when they pushed that idea to the forefront of people's consciousness? You know, special days such as June 1 – Flip a Coin Day, June 13 – Sewing Machine Day, or June 29 – Waffle Iron Day. It may be a challenge to work these special days into a non-profit blog post.

On the other hand, there are summer holidays that make sense to take advantage of. On July 24th, Amelia Earhart Day, you can talk about having a Plan B when things go wrong and do not produce the desired results. On August

7th, National Lighthouse Day, you can write to encourage your readers to highlight their ministry events and progress. On September 6th, Fight Procrastination Day, you could remind people how many opportunities are passed by because we're not getting done what needs to be accomplished.

Of course, if your work is being done outside the US, you could highlight the special days that country celebrates. So, if you're suffering from blogger's block, one idea might be to pull out your calendar, and start thinking about the holidays (special days) coming up and then start writing.

Settling for "Good Enough"

It's not difficult to determine if blogging is something you should continue. Either the readership is building or it's waning. Either readers are engaged and acting, or they're not.

Consistency is a major part of any blog's success. Don't commit to doing too much too soon. Ramp things up gradually.

The question to answer is, "Are the objectives of the blog panning out?" Is the writing causing the desired results?

If you're writing for amusement or to chronicle what's happening, and there are no other goals—then fine. Enjoy yourself.

> **Did you know?**
> Those who prioritize blogging efforts are **13x** more likely to see positive results.

Don't struggle silently. Ask for help. Ask some trusted friends to review your blog strategy and posts to see where things might be improved.

Blog.Grader.com is a free tool that helps identify areas for improvement in a blog.

Here's a good evaluation exercise to look over to assess the blog's value:

Overall

- Does the blog provide information and resources that are not available elsewhere?

- Are analytics being run to track the blog's success?

- Does the blog have a firm publication date, and are posts published on time?

- If you haven't used guest bloggers, is it time?

- Should we continue to post on our regular days, or is there a better time to publish the thoughts?

- Examine other blogs to see how they promote their content.

Audience

- Do readers understand the purpose of the blog?

- Are readers quickly drawn into the conversation?

Format

- Can readers quickly find the articles that interest them most? Are Categories being used?

- Does the blog have a professional look and feel?

- Are "attention-grabbing" headlines used?

Content

- Does the information convey passion and excitement? Is it timely, relevant, interesting, and donor-centric?

- Does the depth of content match the varied needs of the audience?

- Are there links within the text to provide resources that go beyond what's covered?

- Is the content free from spelling, grammatical, and other typographical errors?

- Is the information in the publication "newsworthy?"

- Are there subjects that have not been covered?

- Can the post titles be sharpened to increase interest?

Engagement

- Are readers commenting?

- Are readers sharing the posts with their friends?

- Are the articles what interest the audience most?

- Does the content include information that cannot be found anywhere else?

- Are photos used to build visual interest?

- Are facts being backed up with authority?

- Are people being asked to engage?

Reach

- Can the reader easily share the blog content?

- Are social links included when appropriate?

- Are links provided for readers to gain more insight into the subject being discussed?

- Are influencers being asked to comment?

- Is the content being promoted across the social platforms?

- Are there syndication opportunities that need considering?

The Pros and Cons

It's always worthwhile to look at the tradeoffs before taking on a new assignment. Blogging offers both advantages and disadvantages. Take a moment to look the lists over in advance of deciding whether to start blogging.

Pros and Cons of Blogging	
Pros	**Cons**
• No cost	• Requires attention
• Quick and easy to start	• Takes creativity & originality
• Simplicity	• Needs to be newsworthy
• Living Archive	• May not be the right vehicle
• Readers visit the website	• May be tough to keep going on a regular basis
• Builds loyalty	
• Builds retention	• May cause writer's block
• Results can be measured	• May add unnecessary stress

SHOW & TELL

Blog Promotional Email
Example 1

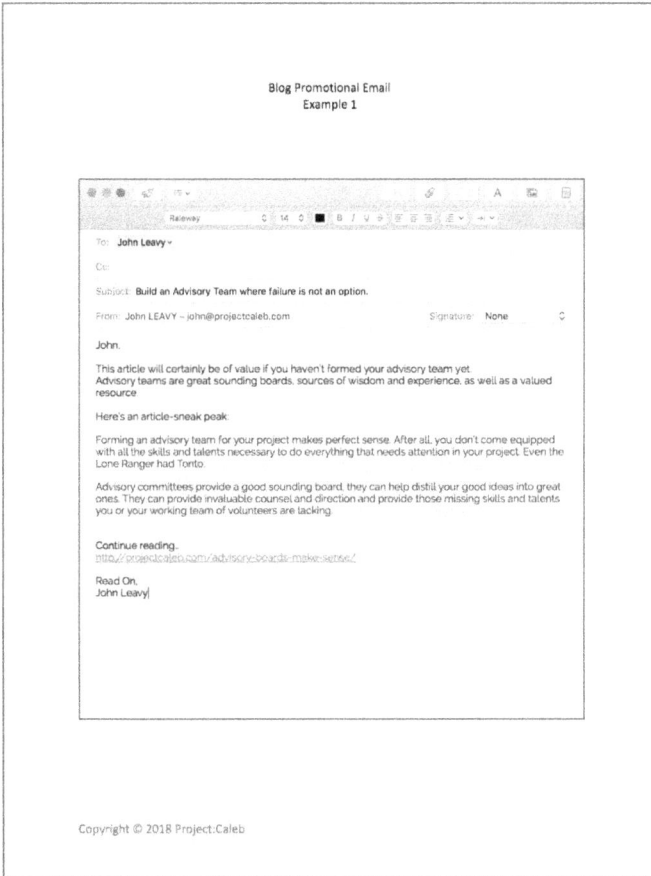

Blog Promotional Email
Example 1

> **To:** John Leavy
>
> **Cc:**
>
> **Subject:** Build an Advisory Team where failure is not an option.
>
> **From:** John LEAVY ~ john@projectcaleb.com   **Signature:** None
>
> John,
>
> This article will certainly be of value if you haven't formed your advisory team yet. Advisory teams are great sounding boards, sources of wisdom and experience, as well as a valued resource.
>
> Here's an article-sneak peak:
>
> Forming an advisory team for your project makes perfect sense. After all, you don't come equipped with all the skills and talents necessary to do everything that needs attention in your project. Even the Lone Ranger had Tonto.
>
> Advisory committees provide a good sounding board, they can help distil your good ideas into great ones. They can provide invaluable counsel and direction and provide those missing skills and talents you or your working team of volunteers are lacking.
>
> Continue reading..
> http://projectcaleb.com/advisory-boards-make-sense/
>
> Read On,
> John Leavy

Copyright © 2018 Project:Caleb

Download at:

johndleavy.com/PC/BlogPromotionalEmail1.pdf

Ignite Your Donor Passion

SHOW & TELL

Blog Promotional Email
Example 2

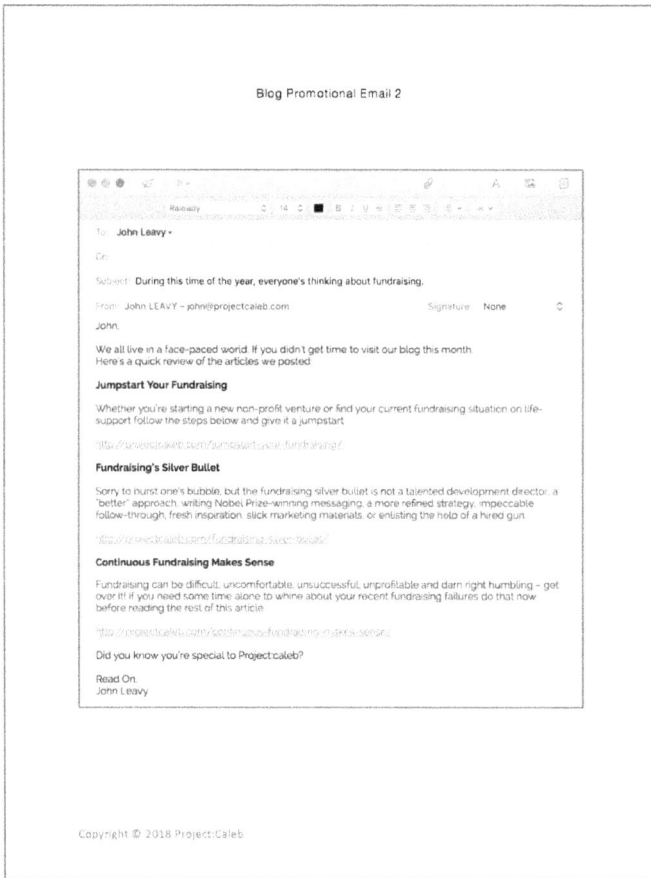

Blog Promotional Email 2

To: John Leavy

Cc:

Subject: During this time of the year, everyone's thinking about fundraising.

From: John LEAVY – john@projectcaleb.com   Signature: None

John,

We all live in a face-paced world. If you didn't get time to visit our blog this month. Here's a quick review of the articles we posted.

Jumpstart Your Fundraising

Whether you're starting a new non-profit venture or find your current fundraising situation on life-support follow the steps below and give it a jumpstart.

http://projectcaleb.com/jumpstart-your-fundraising/

Fundraising's Silver Bullet

Sorry to burst one's bubble, but the fundraising silver bullet is not a talented development director, a "better" approach, writing Nobel Prize-winning messaging, a more refined strategy, impeccable follow-through, fresh inspiration, slick marketing materials, or enlisting the help of a hired gun.

http://projectcaleb.com/fundraisings-silver-bullet/

Continuous Fundraising Makes Sense

Fundraising can be difficult, uncomfortable, unsuccessful, unprofitable and darn right humbling – get over it! If you need some time alone to whine about your recent fundraising failures do that now before reading the rest of this article.

http://projectcaleb.com/continuous-fundraising-makes-sense/

Did you know you're special to Project:caleb?

Read On,
John Leavy

Copyright © 2018 Project:Caleb

Download at:

johndleavy.com/PC/BlogPromotionalEmail2.pdf

FOUR

Create **AMAZING**
Email Messages

E mail still ranks as the fastest, cheapest, and easiest way to communicate with people, whether you need to chat with one person or a small or large group. Of course, nothing will ever surpass the success of the face-to-face experience as the best communication method.

> **Did you know?**
> **205 billion** emails are sent each day. **246 billion** is the expected number by 2019.

Emailing people, such as current supporters and strangers—potential donors, can be triumphantly successful or fraught with disappointment. Sometimes the reasons for lack of success are obvious; other times, the explanations for the shortcomings may be cloudy.

Emails can include a news or support letter. They can showcase current and past blog postings. Or the communique could announce a fundraiser, upcoming meeting, or other event.

Let's start our email examination by looking at the anatomy of an **AMAZING** email message.

> **"Remember, *you're writing to a friend*—**not *your high school English teacher.*"

Next, we'll turn our attention to the strategic reasons for using this short form of communication.

Anatomy of an AMAZING Email Message

Here's a typical email announcing an event:

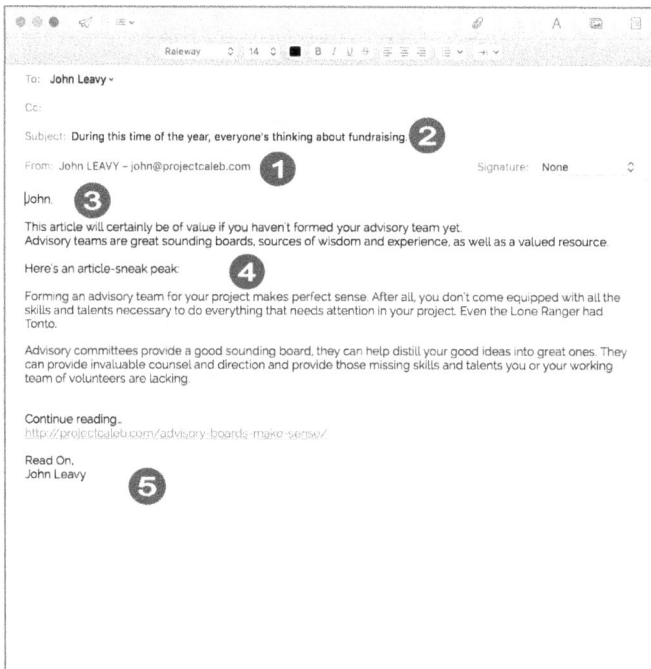

The elementary parts of an email message include Sender, Subject, To, Salutation, Copy (or message), and Signature.

1. **Sender** – People like to hear from people. Think carefully about using the organization's name as the Sender. Also, forget about using no-reply email addresses. Emailing is a two-way street. People want to be able to respond to the person sending the message. When the recipient sees a "no-reply" sender address, they will conclude that the person sending the message does not want to hear back from them.

Did you know?
46% of emails are opened based on the Subject line.

2. **Subject** – DigitalMarketer.com offers eight forms the Subject line might take: Self-interest, Curiosity, Offer, Urgency, Humanity, News, Social Proof, and Story. Let's study an example of each:

Self-interest:

Discover how ministryTHRIVE is transforming the landscape of fundraising.

Curiosity:

More non-profits turn to ministryTHRIVE for fundraising help. Why?

Offer:

Attend a FREE workshop on end-of-the-year fundraising.

Urgency:

Last chance to register...Fundraising Workshop tomorrow.

Humanity:

Caring For The Congo is working to rescue 200 orphans in 2018.

News:

Ghana to become the first developed African country by 2029.

Social Proof:

In 2017, two million people watched the Tour De France on mobile devices.

Story:

Jack thought he lacked the right stuff for his church's mission trip.

> **Did you know?**
> Personalizing the email can boost the open-rate by **270%**.
> (NextAfter.com Experiment #5707)

3. **Salutation** – It's time to retire salutations like: "Dear Friend," "Dear Supporter," "Dear Donor," "Trusted Volunteer," and "Valued Friend," among others. What can be more impersonal than not using the name of the person you're writing to? Make every effort to record the names,

first and last, of each person that crosses your path, whether a potential supporter or regular donor. Start the email by using their first name. If you're writing a person for the first time, perhaps using "Dear" before their first name applies. Dozens or hundreds. If you intend to send out dozens or hundreds of personalized emails, you'll need to use an email automation marketing system such as Mailchimp or Constant Contact. These systems will merge the person's name into what's being sent out. In this way, each email will go out with the person's name as the salutation.

4. **Message** – In Chapter One, *Creating **AMAZING** Donor Passion*, we covered all the ingredients of successful communication. Our focus here is on the copy itself rather than its intent. When writing copy, *less* is always *more*. Say what needs to be said. Say it clearly, be concise, write with passion, and then end the message.

> "Skip using ALL CAPS, **bold letters** and multiple exclamation points!!!!— say it with words not punctuation."

5. **Signature** – When the message is being sent to a friend, do you really use an image of your signature, followed by a bunch of social icons, and a favorite quote or verse-of-the-day? Or do you simply sign off using your first name? The message is being sent to a friend, a colleague, or an

associate. Skip all the templates and branding stuff. Just be yourself.

6. **Attachments** – Unfortunately, some nefarious individuals use email attachments to spread viruses on unsuspecting recipients' computers. These days, many people will not open an email attachment for that very reason. A better option would be to upload the file, whether it's a video, newsletter, or something else, to your website and then add a link in the email. People receiving the message with a link are more likely to download the file.

Did you know?
54% of emails are opened on mobile devices.

Developing an Email Strategy

Several key components comprise a sound email strategy: selecting the target audience, choosing the appropriate delivery platform, determining the message, crafting the copy, selecting the timeframe, executing the campaign, and measuring the success of the efforts. Let's examine each:

Choosing an Audience – It doesn't make sense to send the same message out to every potential giver and current donor. They have different interests. They're at various commitment levels and have dissimilar relationships with the organization.

Besides, how will we know what's working and what's not if the same message is sent to all 3,000 people in our contact file?

The section titled, *Segmenting Your Audience* in Chapter One discusses creating *personas* to differentiate between the various potential supporters and donors. In this way, a person can send tailored email messages geared to each group's interests and specialize the message to what each group wants to hear.

Deciding on the Right Delivery Channel – The only way to gauge the success of an email campaign is to track the number of people who receive, open, and act on (click-throughs) the message being sent. To achieve this, an email marketing automation system such as Mailchimp or Constant Contact needs to be utilized. Mailchimp offers a free plan for users sending emails to fewer than 2,000 contacts. Constant Contact has a 60-day free trial. Both offerings feature numerous examples, training, and expert advice.

Settling on the Message – Potential givers need to be educated and nurtured over time before they will likely signal their support for the work being done.

Donors, on the other hand, have already said, "yes" to being part of the effort. They require a deeper understanding of the progress being made, the impact the organization is gaining, and a knowledge of how the funds are being expended.

The email messages going out need to be tailored to each group's interests and passions.

Did you know?
Email open-rates jump by **39%** when segmenting the list of recipients.

Note: Check out "Telling a Great Story" in the first book in the Ignition Series titled **Ignite Your End-of-the-year Fundraising***.*

Crafting the Copy – The message within the email typically serves one of five purposes: to inform, educate, engage, inspire, or prompt action. Before sending out the emails, decide on the goal of the communique. What is it we want the message to achieve? What is it we want the reader to do? How will we determine its success or failure?

Selecting the Timing – Email campaigns require a strategic approach when it comes to sending messages at the optimal time and interval. "At the last minute," never works as an effective tactic. If the contact file contains 5,000 names, send half of the emails in the morning and the other half in the afternoon. See which emails receive the best results. Try the same tactic as the day of the week. Monday or Tuesday may be the best time to attract potential donors' attention. Over time, settle into a system that works best for the organization.

Executing the Campaign – During the execution phase, we'll want to closely monitor the success rate of the email campaign. This is where email marketing automation systems, such as Constant Contact or Mailchimp, are of great value. These systems can help determine how the email campaign is proceeding and if success is within our grasp.

Consistency is a linchpin to any effective email campaign. If the monthly newsletter typically goes out on the first Tuesday of each month, then do everything within your power to make sure the publication goes out on time. If a series of emails is going out over 21 days, then stick to the schedule. Consistency helps build the reader's expectations.

Here are four email campaign examples:

<u>*Campaign 1:*</u>

In this first example, an appeal letter is printed out and sent by US Mail. Of course, the letter is given to someone in person or enclosed within an email.

Find all four-letter Examples at the end of this chapter.

Campaign 2:

An email can be sent with just a snippet of the current issue, or it may include the entire newsletter. Then, if the whole newsletter is posted on the website or blog, it gives people a reason to visit the site. In this campaign example, the whole newsletter is sent to recipients via Mailchimp.

Campaign 3:

In this campaign example, the message announces the latest blog posting. It should grab the reader's attention and be brief. Consider including the title of the piece, a brief introductory paragraph, and a link that encourages readers to visit the blog to continue reading.

Don't include the whole story in the email, or people will have no reason to visit the blog, read other articles, or explore the website.

Campaign 4:

In this example, four emails are sent over 21 days.
The first email is sent out 21 days before the event. In this case, a workshop on fundraising. The event could be any occurrence, such as a workday, a race, a golf tournament, or a benefit concert.

The second email outlines a portion of the event that would be of interest to a large part of the audience. This message is sent 14 days before the workshop.

The third email is sent out 7 days before the workshop, highlighting another subject that will interest most attendees.

The last email is sent out 24 hours before the event—a previous attempt to register some stragglers.

The key is to find the correct number of touches (emails to send). We don't want to send out too few messages, nor do we wish to aggravate recipients with a large number.

Boosting Your Email Open-Rate

Let's say we want to increase the open-rate of the emails we send to our current donor file. How is that accomplished? Let's examine the factors that affect the open-rate and develop some strategies to increase the percentage of emails opened.

> **Did you know?**
> Removing the organization's name from the Sender
> line increased the open-rate by **18%**.
> (NextAfter.com Experiment #5930)

Have a Clean List of Names – The first step might be to ensure the donor file or contact list is up to date. Over time, the names of individuals who have repeatedly failed to replay should be removed. Some organizations would say this suggestion borders on heresy. But what good does it do to have a donor file of 2,000 names when only 1,300 people have indicated they want to hear from us?

Personalization Makes a Big Difference – Let's look at three areas where personalization can make a massive difference in the open-rate. First, we have the sender's name. People like to hear from individuals, so ensure the email sender's name is a person's name, not the name of the organization. Tinker with the sender's name if the emails have been coming from the president of the organization. The email recipients may not believe the leader of the organization has the time to communicate with them. Perhaps the email should come from the fundraising chairperson or another key person within the organization. Second, we've already covered that personalizing the recipient's name dramatically improves the open-rate. Make every effort to secure the names of people interested in the organization's work. Forget using "Dear Supporter," "Dear Friend," "Dear Donor," and the rest of the tired lot. The last factor deals with the signature at the end of the message. Surely, you do not use an image of your signature when sending an email to a friend or family member. Stay personal and just sign off using your first or full name, depending on the relationship you have with the person.

One Message Does Not Fit All – We've also discussed how segmenting the list increases the open-rate by 39%. Potential supporters and donors are looking for different information. Potential supporters need to be informed, educated, and nurtured until they are ready to decide if they want to support the organization. Donors are looking for information on how their gifts are being used and what impact is being made from their participation.

Be Mobile-Friendly – Additionally, 54% of emails are opened on mobile devices. Emails being sent today must be mobile-friendly, or the chances of them being opened are limited.

Ask for Permission – Don't forget the section titled, *Ask for Permission—Don't Assume* in Chapter ONE. We must communicate with the people who want to hear from us. If we don't, the open-rate will be skewed and we'll annoy people by filling their inboxes with unwanted emails.

Grab the Reader's Attention – Ensure the first sentence captivates the reader and clearly conveys the purpose of the communication. Don't assume people want to read what's being sent.

> "*Successful email campaigns eventually stall out—**Make moderate changes until the results start to turn around.**"*

Timing Is Everything – The timing of sending out the emails has already been discussed. Always keep exploring this element to ensure the best day and time for sending out the emails is still applicable.

The Subject – The Subject is one of the seminal factors in piquing a person's interest enough to cause them to open an email. Don't write haphazard subject lines. Make a concerted effort to ensure the theme is as engaging as possible.

Do A/B Testing – One strategy is to create different subject lines and send them to segment groups. If we had a contact file of 1,000 names, we could divide the group into two parts and send out two email groups with different subject lines to see which one caused more opens.

> *"Email marketing gives an organization the ability to test, test, test until they find a message that works."*

Converting Recipients into Subscribers and Donors

Converting recipients into subscribers and donors takes distinct levels of commitment. People who subscribe to a newsletter make one level of commitment, while those who give to an organization show a much higher level of commitment. We've already discussed the fact that potential supporters and donors are seeking diverse types of information and attention.

When executing a typical email campaign, the results usually fall into four buckets:

- People who open the email and act

- People who open the email, who may or may not read it, and take no action
- People who do not open the email
- People who unsubscribe from future email deliveries

People who open the email and act – our job is done. Success was secured.

People who open the email, who may or may not read it, and take no action. For those who opened the email and did not act, we can assume the email was not of interest, or that our timing in sending them the information was not optimal. Making several changes could improve the open-rate. We could try a new subject line. We could adjust the content to see if we can create more interest. The emails could be sent out at a different time or on a different day. We could change the sender's name.

People who unsubscribe from future email deliveries – The reality is, some people will unsubscribe. Yes, even family and friends may not want to receive the communiques. Be understanding and let their decision stand without comment.

Now that we've addresses the mechanics of converting recipients into subscribers and donors, let's examine the role of the content enclosed within the email in more detail.

A subscriber is someone who demonstrates an interest in the organization's mission. This person may have provided their email address to receive a free eBook, subscribed to a newsletter, or chosen to follow the organization on its social media platform. This person has shown an initial level of interest. Now they need to be further informed, educated, engaged, and nurtured to determine if they might want to be involved at a higher level.

Once donors, the recipients will want more details on what's happening. They'll want to know how the funds are being used and whether a real impact on people's lives is taking place. They'll be more interested in the organization's long-range plans.

The content for both groups needs to be directed toward what interests them most.

Measuring Success

Measuring the Success of Your Efforts – If the open-rate of the initial email is low, whether you send one email or a series, then perhaps the content needs to be adjusted or enhanced. Maybe the day or time the emails are sent needs further consideration. Don't continue to send out the messages, hoping for the results to improve. Make changes. Be proactive.

Focus on the numbers that matter most. It's great to have a contact file of thousands of names. But how many of those people want to hear from you? It's great that the open-rate for the email campaign is 10 points above the national non-profit average for your sector. But is the readership acting? Are they subscribing? Joining? Giving? The action taking place cannot only be on your part. People need to show interest—in the form of action.

Did you know?

Organizations should adhere to the CAN-SPAM Act of 2003 by giving recipients the option of opting out or unsubscribing to the email.

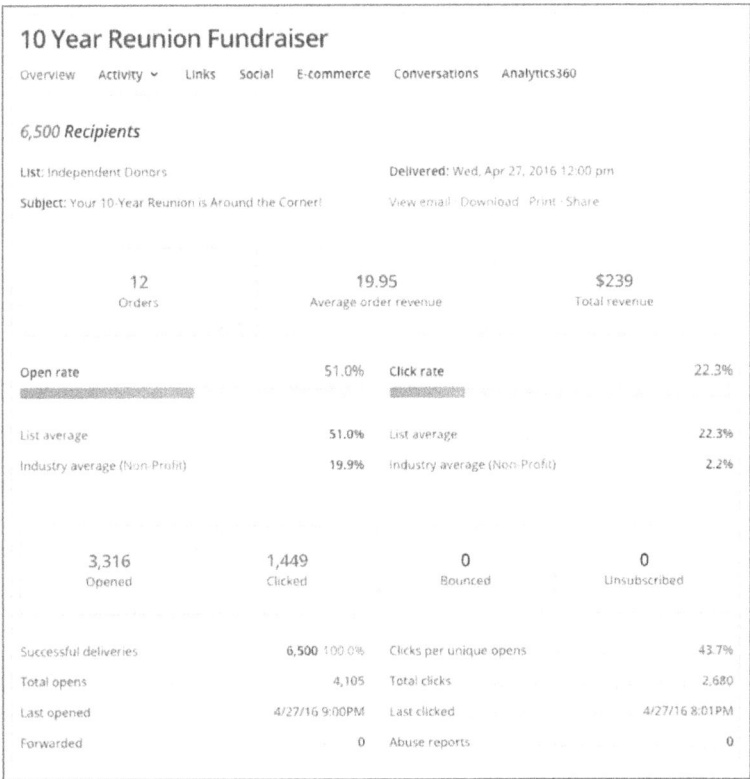

10 Year Reunion Fundraiser

Overview   Activity ⌄   Links   Social   E-commerce   Conversations   Analytics360

6,500 Recipients

List: Independent Donors

Subject: Your 10-Year Reunion is Around the Corner!

Delivered: Wed, Apr 27, 2016 12:00 pm

View email · Download · Print · Share

12	19.95	$239
Orders	Average order revenue	Total revenue

Open rate	51.0%	Click rate	22.3%
List average	51.0%	List average	22.3%
Industry average (Non-Profit)	19.9%	Industry average (Non-Profit)	2.2%

3,316	1,449	0	0
Opened	Clicked	Bounced	Unsubscribed

Successful deliveries	6,500 100.0%	Clicks per unique opens	43.7%
Total opens	4,105	Total clicks	2,680
Last opened	4/27/16 9:00PM	Last clicked	4/27/16 8:01PM
Forwarded	0	Abuse reports	0

Using a marketing automation service such as Mailchimp gives you the ability to track the recipient's reaction to what's sent. Above is a snapshot of Mailchimp's Overview page:

This page provides us with a wealth of information on how the campaign was run. Six thousand five hundred people received the email, while three thousand three hundred sixteen opened the message—that makes the open-rate 51%. The industry average is only 19.9%. The click-through rate was 22.3%. It appears 12 people have placed orders.

Information like this is invaluable. Without these statistics, organizations would be left to guess at the success of their email campaigns.

To gain a good understanding of how email campaigns run, it is important to dissect the message into its main components to identify what's failing. Here's a set of questions to consider:

1. Is the email being sent out to a current (fresh/accurate) list of potential supporters or current donors?
2. Has the best time to send the email been determined?
3. Is the Sender's name appropriate?
4. Does the Subject pique interest?
5. Is the opening personalized?
6. Is the purpose of the message obvious and well-stated?
7. Is the copy compelling?

8. Is there a strong call to action?

9. Again, is the closing personalized?

Answering these questions will help the next campaign garner better results.

Settling for "Good Enough"

Should we ever settle for "good enough?" Possibly not. This is God's work we're about after all. Suppose we set out to raise $30,000, and we ended up raising $40,000. What if we wanted to add 100 new email addresses to our contact file so we could nurture and engage these potential donors over the coming months? Should we be satisfied with 100? What if our email open-rate is twice the national average for a non-profit in our industry? Should we stop trying to do better?

If you Google the search term "continuous improvement," you'll find over 36 million occurrences. That means there are quite a few people, surely millions, not satisfied with "good enough" or "looks like we made it."

Here's a list of ways to build an organization's email list. You'll have to be the judge of which ones you believe are the best fit.

- Utilize social media platform, like Facebook, Instagram, or Pinterest to collect new email addresses.

- Swap email addresses with like-minded organizations.

- Buy email addresses from list brokers.

- Ask current donors to share or forward your information to others.

- Guest blog on popular sites and include a call to action.

- Write an article for the local newspaper or another publication and encourage the readership to visit your website.

- Secure an interview on a local radio station and ask the listeners to email in their comments and questions.

- Speak at small gatherings (Sunday School classes, small groups, mission committees, or Bible studies) and collect people's contact information.

- Network. Network. Network.

Here's a good email evaluation exercise to look over:

Overall

- Should we continue to search for the optimal day and time to send out the messages?
- Would it make a difference if the emails were sent by someone else in the organization?

- Is the purpose of the email obvious?

- Is an email automation program, such as Mailchimp or Constant Contact, being used to track the email's success rate?

- Are there other people we can bring into the discussions on evaluating our email process?

Audience

- Do the readers understand the purposes of the emails?

- Are the messages customized per audience segment?

- Is one audience segment showing more interest than another?

Format

- Does the email format fit the audience?

- Are the images telling a story?

- Does using a template or plain text format work better?

Content

- Is the subject matter donor-centric?

- Does the Subject inspire people to open the message?

- Are the emails the right length?

- If the emails are being used as an appeal mechanism, are the calls to action obvious and understandable?

- If the purposes of the emails are to drive people to the website or blog, is that working out?

- Should the copy be reordered?

- Are there ways the story could be made more compelling or impactful?

Engagement

- Can the Subject lines be sharpened to increase the open-rate?

- Do the calls to action trigger people to act?

- Are the emails using the social sharing button?

- Are supporters or donors engaging with the messages being sent?

- Are the recipients replying positively?

- Are different types of emails being sent to trigger increased engagement?

Reach

- Are recipients being encouraged to share the email contents if appropriate?

- Is social content being used in emails to encourage recipients to follow the organization's social media presence?

- Is reach being tracked?

- Are the emails being promoted on the other organization's platforms?

- Is the blog's content being promoted?

The Pros and Cons

Most of the time, examining the pros and cons of a new project helps make the decision easier. Peruse the following list:

Pros and Cons of Emailing	
Pros	**Cons**
• Inexpensive	• May be lost in the crowd
• Short Start time	• May be seen as SPAM
• Targeted audience	• May limit originality
• Sharpen message	• May be seen as intrusive
• Builds loyalty	• May not be the right vehicle
• Builds retention	• May be tough to keep going on a regular basis
• Personalization	• May lack information to share
• Results can be measured	

Several statistics in this chapter courtesy of: *A Data-driven Guide to Email Marketing Strategy,* posted by Steven MacDonald on September 5, 2017.

SHOW & TELL

Appeal Letter
Example (1)

---

project:caleb

Date: November 16, 2025

Dear John,

**Did you know that 50% of ministries and non-profits never raise more than $10,000?
82% fail to raise their first $100,000.**

Why?

These leaders love people, love ministry, and love God. The plain truth is they lack the fundamental experience of getting their ministry off the ground—they don't know where to begin when developing and executing a fundraising strategy that produces positive results.

Project: Caleb has taken on the task of providing solid, sound information to the leader.

We launched a series of instructional books titled the Ignition Series. The first book, **Ignite Your End-of-the-year Fundraising**, is available now on Amazon.com and wherever books are sold.

Ignite Your Donor Passion is scheduled for release this December, followed by **Ignite Your Year-round Fundraising** (a look at raising funds all year long) in March 2018.

The Ignition Series is packed with information, experience, wisdom, examples, and handouts. Here are a few comments from ministry leaders:

> "Well organized, easy to follow, and a must-read for small to medium-sized charities." – Greg Smith, Director of Operations, New Horizons Foundations

> "Ignite Your End-of-the-year Fundraising will give you a fresh look at your year-end priorities and plans. Like all of Leavy's books, this book is full of practical wisdom and clear steps for your take-away." – John Shelhamer, President, Development Testing Services

We believe the best way and most economical avenue to make ministries aware of this book series is to conduct presentations and workshops at national conferences.

The first conference we have targeted is the Association of Gospel Rescue Mission's "Walk in Wisdom" convention, held in Milwaukee from June 12 to 15, 2018.

The Association of Gospel Rescue Missions (AGRM) has already extended an invitation for us to speak at their national gathering in 2018.

Copyright © 2025 John D. Leavy

Download at:

johndleavy.com/PC/AppealLetterExample.pdf

SHOW &TELL

Appeal Letter
Example (2)

Paying for the trip will be challenging. Project Caleb has not appealed for support in the past, but perhaps God has other plans.

Here's what the trip will cost:

- Join AGRM's Business Partners - $440/annual fee
- Airfare – $382 (of course, this changes minute-by-minute)
- Hotel – $129 per night for four nights
- Conference registration – $489 (early-bird registration ends 12/15)

The total cost is $1,827. Would you consider sponsoring a portion of this trip or perhaps a single item, such as the plane fare or conference fee?

Like King David, when raising funds for the building of the temple, I have donated the first $200.

Join in this venture, be blessed, and in turn, bless others.

Donations can be made online at joytotheworldfoundation.org. Just search for Project Caleb and click the "DONATE NOW TO THIS PROJECT" button on our donation page. This is a tax-deductible donation.

As a "Thank You" for your gift, we would like to send you a copy of **Ignite Your End-of-the-Fundraising** ($12.95) and **Ignite Your Donor Passion** ($19.95).

Be in prayer as God works this out.

I'm looking forward to sharing the exciting details of the Milwaukee trip after attending.

Look to Him,
John

Copyright © 2025 John D. Leavy

Download at:

Johndleavy.com/PCAppealLetterExample.pdf

SHOW &TELL

Newsletter w/Email Example (1)

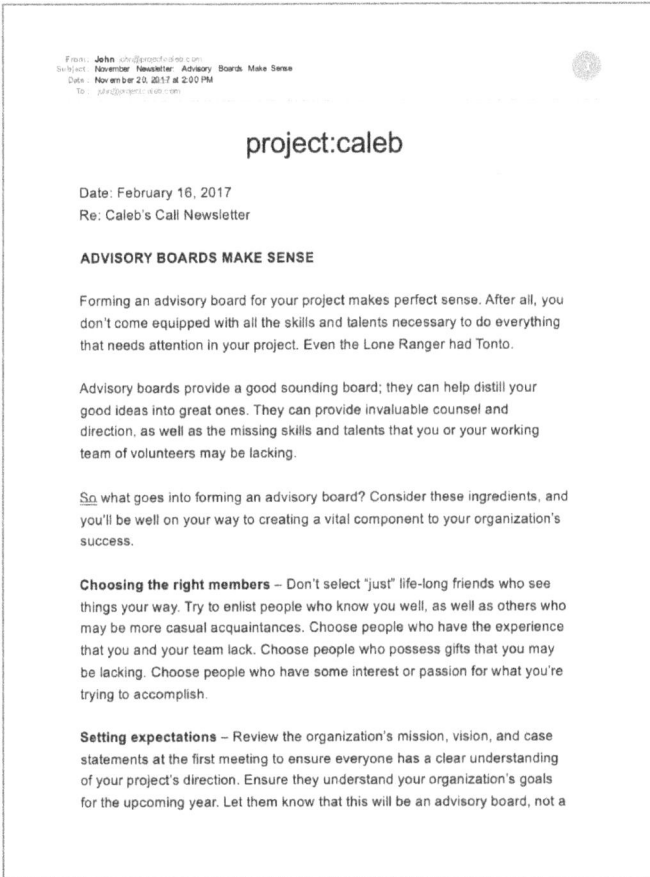

From: **John** john@projectcaleb.com
Subject: November Newsletter Advisory Boards Make Sense
Date: November 20, 2017 at 2:00 PM
To: john@projectcaleb.com

project:caleb

Date: February 16, 2017
Re: Caleb's Call Newsletter

ADVISORY BOARDS MAKE SENSE

Forming an advisory board for your project makes perfect sense. After all, you don't come equipped with all the skills and talents necessary to do everything that needs attention in your project. Even the Lone Ranger had Tonto.

Advisory boards provide a good sounding board; they can help distill your good ideas into great ones. They can provide invaluable counsel and direction, as well as the missing skills and talents that you or your working team of volunteers may be lacking.

So what goes into forming an advisory board? Consider these ingredients, and you'll be well on your way to creating a vital component to your organization's success.

Choosing the right members – Don't select "just" life-long friends who see things your way. Try to enlist people who know you well, as well as others who may be more casual acquaintances. Choose people who have the experience that you and your team lack. Choose people who possess gifts that you may be lacking. Choose people who have some interest or passion for what you're trying to accomplish.

Setting expectations – Review the organization's mission, vision, and case statements at the first meeting to ensure everyone has a clear understanding of your project's direction. Ensure they understand your organization's goals for the upcoming year. Let them know that this will be an advisory board, not a

---

Download at:

johndleavy.com/PC/NewsletterEmailExample.pdf

SHOW & TELL

Newsletter w/Email Example (2)

working board. On the other hand, if the board will be a "working" board, then set everyone's expectations by assigning responsibilities and try your best to gauge the amount of time people will need to commit to each month. An agenda should be emailed two weeks before each board meeting, allowing board members sufficient time to prepare their thoughts. Minutes of the meeting should also be sent out the week after the gathering so people can track what was discussed.

Defining responsibilities – Let people know upfront what you're expecting them to commit to, such as a one-year commitment or attending three 90-minute breakfast meetings per year. There will be no homework and nothing to bring to each meeting. You're just looking for sound counsel and advice.

Picking a convenient time and place – Choose a meeting place that is as convenient and neutral as possible. A comfortable room at church (a fireplace would be a great add-on), a standard room at a community center, or even your own living room or kitchen table may help inspire conversation. For example, our advisory board meets three times a year, in February, May, and October. This was intentional to avoid summer and holiday meeting times. The meetings last only 90 minutes – no marathon get-togethers that wear people out.

Doing the "ask" in person – Emails and phone calls will not be as effective as face-to-face meetings over a cup of coffee. This brief gathering provides an opportunity for you to share your passion and mission. The person listening can see your composure. Once people sense your enthusiasm for the project, they may opt in, even if they're busy. Make sure to follow up even if they decide to join or tell you they're schedule won't permit it.

Financially supporting the vision – Some operating projects believe it is essential for those on the board to provide financial support for the efforts. It's a decision that should be made before asking people to be involved. It makes sense on several levels for board members to be financially engaged in the work. Say, for instance, if those on the board will be involved in fundraising. A conversation with a potential donor might become uncomfortable if the board

Download at:

johndleavy.com/PC/NewsletterEmailExample.pdf

SHOW & TELL

Newsletter w/Email Example (3)

member were asked if they support the mission. Having board members support the mission will undoubtedly cause them to have a closer tie to the success of what's happening as well.

Giving each person an out – Not everyone will have the necessary bandwidth, even if you're just asking them to attend a few breakfast meetings each year.
Be gracious enough and provide them an easy out if they cannot commit.

If your organization or project does not have an advisory board, consider adding this item to your list of goals for 2016. Good luck.

This email was sent to john@projectcaleb.com
Why did I get this? unsubscribe from this list update subscription preferences
Project Caleb · 1558 Portland Gold Drive · Colorado Springs, CO 80905 · USA

MailChimp

Download at:

johndleavy.com/PC/NewsletterEmailExample.pdf

SHOW & TELL

Blog Promotional Email Example

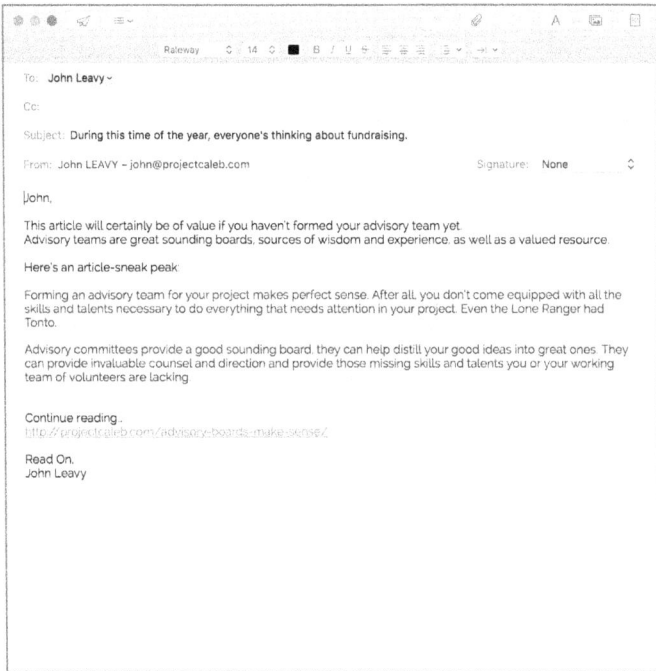

To: John Leavy ˅

Cc:

Subject: During this time of the year, everyone's thinking about fundraising.

From: John LEAVY – john@projectcaleb.com   Signature: None   ˅

John,

This article will certainly be of value if you haven't formed your advisory team yet.
Advisory teams are great sounding boards, sources of wisdom and experience, as well as a valued resource.

Here's an article-sneak peak:

Forming an advisory team for your project makes perfect sense. After all, you don't come equipped with all the skills and talents necessary to do everything that needs attention in your project. Even the Lone Ranger had Tonto.

Advisory committees provide a good sounding board, they can help distill your good ideas into great ones. They can provide invaluable counsel and direction and provide those missing skills and talents you or your working team of volunteers are lacking.

Continue reading .
http://projectcaleb.com/advisory-boards-make-sense/

Read On,
John Leavy

Download at:

johndleavy.com/PC/BlogPromotionalEmail1.pdf

Event Promotional Email Series Example 1

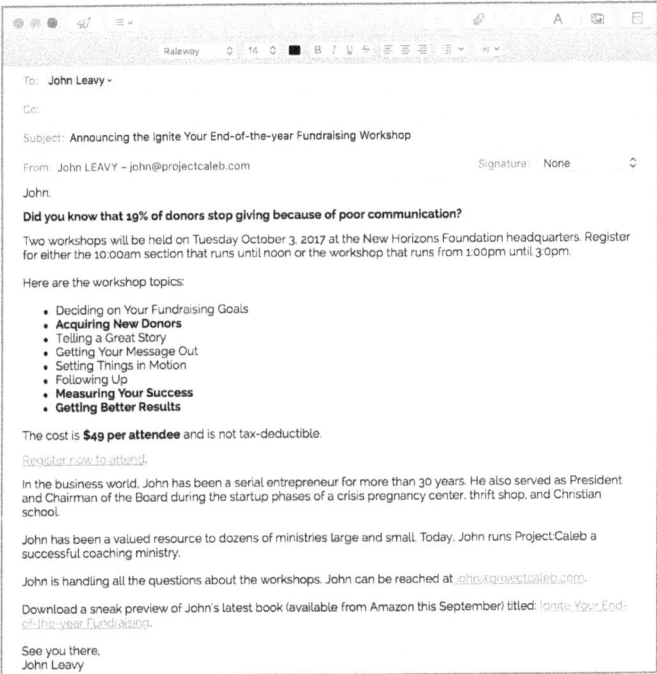

To: John Leavy ˅

Cc:

Subject: Announcing the Ignite Your End-of-the-year Fundraising Workshop

From: John LEAVY – john@projectcaleb.com   Signature: None

John,

Did you know that 19% of donors stop giving because of poor communication?

Two workshops will be held on Tuesday October 3, 2017 at the New Horizons Foundation headquarters. Register for either the 10:00am section that runs until noon or the workshop that runs from 1:00pm until 3:0pm.

Here are the workshop topics:

- Deciding on Your Fundraising Goals
- **Acquiring New Donors**
- Telling a Great Story
- Getting Your Message Out
- Setting Things in Motion
- Following Up
- **Measuring Your Success**
- **Getting Better Results**

The cost is **$49 per attendee** and is not tax-deductible.

Register now to attend.

In the business world, John has been a serial entrepreneur for more than 30 years. He also served as President and Chairman of the Board during the startup phases of a crisis pregnancy center, thrift shop, and Christian school.

John has been a valued resource to dozens of ministries large and small. Today, John runs Project:Caleb a successful coaching ministry.

John is handling all the questions about the workshops. John can be reached at john@projectcaleb.com.

Download a sneak preview of John's latest book (available from Amazon this September) titled: Ignite Your End-of-the-year Fundraising.

See you there,
John Leavy

Download at:

johndleavy.com/PC/EventPromotionalEmail1.pdf

SHOW & TELL

Event Promotional Email Series
Example 2

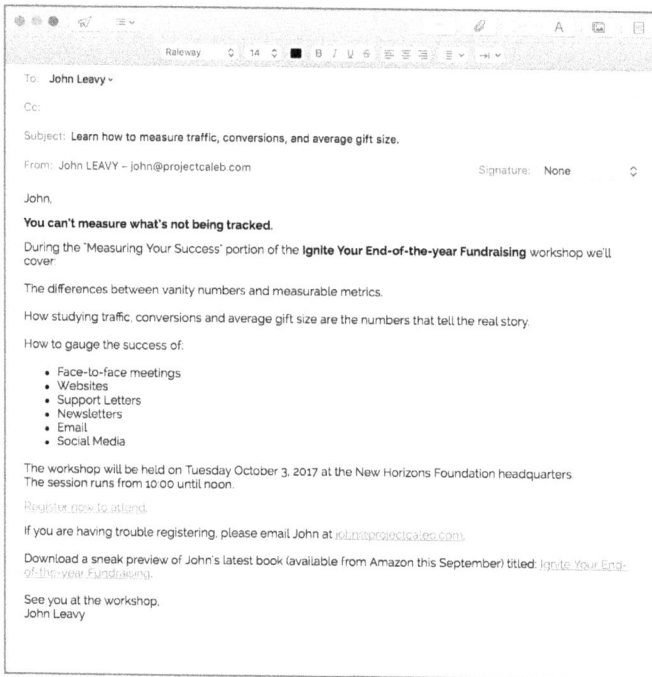

To: John Leavy

Cc:

Subject: Learn how to measure traffic, conversions, and average gift size.

From: John LEAVY – john@projectcaleb.com   Signature: None

John,

You can't measure what's not being tracked.

During the "Measuring Your Success" portion of the **Ignite Your End-of-the-year Fundraising** workshop we'll cover:

The differences between vanity numbers and measurable metrics.

How studying traffic, conversions and average gift size are the numbers that tell the real story.

How to gauge the success of:

- Face-to-face meetings
- Websites
- Support Letters
- Newsletters
- Email
- Social Media

The workshop will be held on Tuesday October 3, 2017 at the New Horizons Foundation headquarters. The session runs from 10:00 until noon.

Register now to attend.

If you are having trouble registering, please email John at john@projectcaleb.com.

Download a sneak preview of John's latest book (available from Amazon this September) titled: Ignite Your End-of-the-year Fundraising.

See you at the workshop.
John Leavy

Download at:

johndleavy.com/PC/EventPromotionalEmail2.pdf

SHOW & TELL

Event Promotional Email Series Example 3

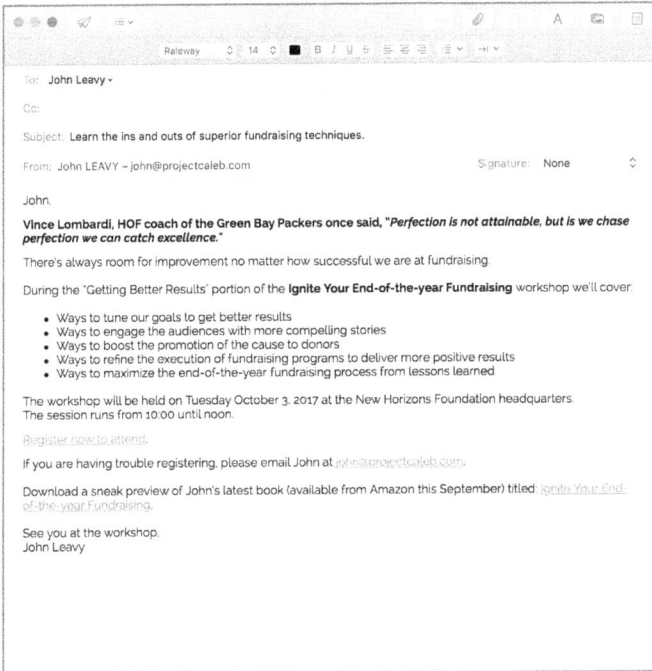

To: John Leavy ▾

Cc:

Subject: Learn the ins and outs of superior fundraising techniques.

From: John LEAVY – john@projectcaleb.com   Signature: None ⇕

John.

Vince Lombardi, HOF coach of the Green Bay Packers once said, *"Perfection is not attainable, but is we chase perfection we can catch excellence."*

There's always room for improvement no matter how successful we are at fundraising.

During the "Getting Better Results" portion of the **Ignite Your End-of-the-year Fundraising** workshop we'll cover:

- Ways to tune our goals to get better results
- Ways to engage the audiences with more compelling stories
- Ways to boost the promotion of the cause to donors
- Ways to refine the execution of fundraising programs to deliver more positive results
- Ways to maximize the end-of-the-year fundraising process from lessons learned

The workshop will be held on Tuesday October 3, 2017 at the New Horizons Foundation headquarters. The session runs from 10:00 until noon.

Register now to attend.

If you are having trouble registering, please email John at john@projectcaleb.com.

Download a sneak preview of John's latest book (available from Amazon this September) titled: Ignite Your End-of-the-year Fundraising.

See you at the workshop.
John Leavy

Download at:

johndleavy.com/PC/EventPromotionalEmail3.pdf

SHOW & TELL

Event Promotional Email Series
Example 4

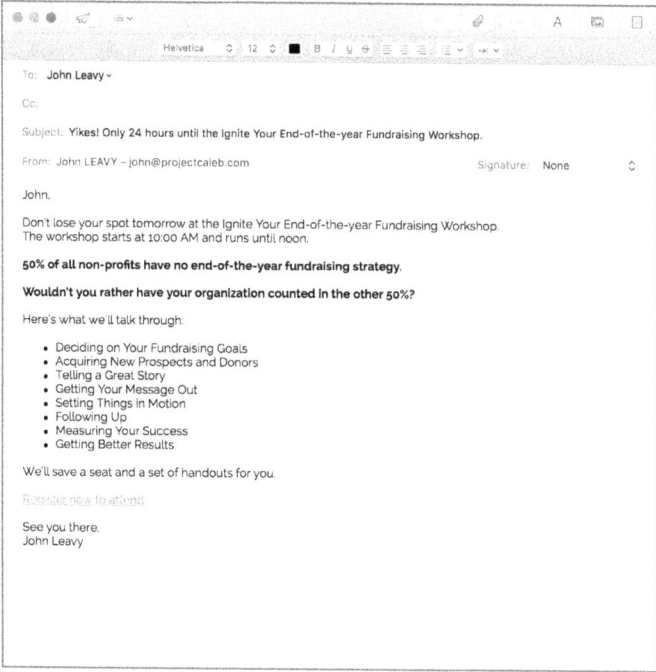

To: John Leavy ⌄

Cc:

Subject: Yikes! Only 24 hours until the Ignite Your End-of-the-year Fundraising Workshop.

From: John LEAVY – john@projectcaleb.com   Signature: None ⌄

John,

Don't lose your spot tomorrow at the Ignite Your End-of-the-year Fundraising Workshop. The workshop starts at 10:00 AM and runs until noon.

50% of all non-profits have no end-of-the-year fundraising strategy.

Wouldn't you rather have your organization counted in the other 50%?

Here's what we'll talk through:

- Deciding on Your Fundraising Goals
- Acquiring New Prospects and Donors
- Telling a Great Story
- Getting Your Message Out
- Setting Things in Motion
- Following Up
- Measuring Your Success
- Getting Better Results

We'll save a seat and a set of handouts for you.

Register now to attend

See you there.
John Leavy

Download at:

johndleavy.com/PC/EventPromotionalEmail4.pdf

FIVE

(15 MIN READ)

Create **AMAZING**
Newsletters

Newsletters can be short or long. They can focus on a single subject or have a broader scope. The writing can be in-depth or brief. The format may be in plain text or designed using a sleek template. The publication may be loaded with links to click on, plus scores of interesting images. The stories might range from informative to educational or promotional. The publication may be released on. a weekly, monthly, or irregular basis. Newsletters could be sent out electronically by email or through the US Mail.

If you're considering this type of publication, let's look at the ingredients that contribute to an **AMAZING** newsletter, glance at a newsletter's anatomy, and then shift our attention to the strategic reasons for turning out the publication.

> *"Before jumping into publishing a newsletter, ask yourself—**Is a newsletter for me; do I like to write?**"*

Anatomy of an AMAZING Newsletter

Let's break down the parts of this promotional newsletter piece:

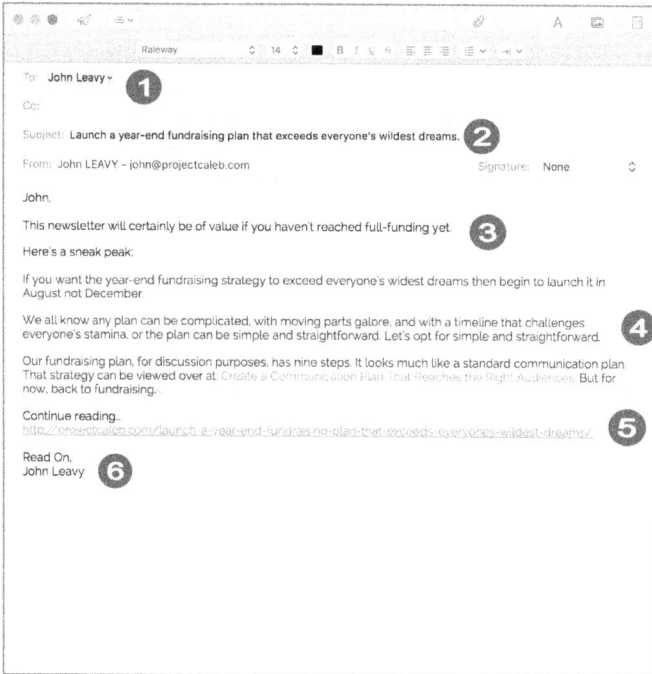

1. **To** – Personalize the email.

2. **Subject** – Make sure the subject piques the recipient's interest.

3. **Purpose** – The purpose must be clear and engaging for the reader to continue.

4. **Content** – Include just enough content so the reader knows what the newsletter contains. Leave out the balance to create some intrigue and encourage them to visit the blog.

5. **Call to action** – Tell people to continue reading. Don't assume they'll go to the blog without being told.

6. **Closing** – Use a personal close. Always keep the dialogue friendly.

Developing a Newsletter Strategy

Mission would be the first element to tackle. Why invest the necessary time, resources, and talent? Newsletters are resource hogs, time bandits. What if it were decided that the mission of the newsletter was two-fold: first, to inform, educate, engage, and second, to begin to build relationships that lead readers to become involved in the organization's work.

Purpose is the next ingredient to explore. The *mission* is what we do, and the *purpose* is why we do it. Wired Impact is an organization that builds websites for non-profits. They believe the Internet is a tool that is to be used for good. They further surmise that relationships make more things happen. Their job focuses on empowering the non-profits they work with, and they believe tangible results should drive everything they do.

Knowing the Audience is the cornerstone of any publication's success. What does the reader think is relevant or, important? What problems do they believe need solving? What are they passionate about seeing happen? How do they measure impact, success? The writer must know what the reader wants to see happen.

> *"I have made this longer than usual because I have not had the time to make it shorter."* — Blaise Pascal

Attention-grabbing Headlines ensure the publication is read. Craft, craft, and recraft the story headlines to make sure they immediately grab the reader's attention. It takes more time and attention to make headlines succinic. The stories, no matter how interesting or noteworthy, won't be read if the headlines never draw the reader into the story.

Did you know?
Organizations choose email **66%** of the time as their preferred method to send newsletters.

Newsworthy means what's being shared is: interesting, notable, important, significant, momentous, historic, remarkable, sensational, unprecedented, groundbreaking. Newsworthy does not mean one person knows something another individual does not.

Offer Value to the readership to keep them coming back. Does the publication answer a question, build relationships, serve an audience, address a need, solve a problem, encourage participation or action, inspire engagement, or rally the troops? The reader is spending the time reading the publication. What are they receiving in return?

The **Format** of the newsletter needs to serve the needs of both the writer and its readership. The publication may be short or long. It may have one story or several features. Will it be branded? What fonts and images should be used? Should links be used to send readers to more information, the organization's website, or social page?

The **Layout** of the publication is also important. Should the newsletter use a template or be written in plain text? Should it be done in a magazine or newspaper style? Will all the headlines be at the top of the publication with links to the balance of the stories for quick access? Should readers be sent to the organization's blog to read the rest of the accounts?

Correct Timing can build or break a publication. Will the newsletter go to press weekly, monthly, or quarterly? Know your limitations. Start slow, then increase your efforts as interest and circulation build. Monthly may be the perfect timeframe.

Consistency raises people's expectations and creates anticipation and interest. Set a publication schedule and stick to it.

Everyone's time and attention are being strained today. If readers know the newsletter comes out on the first Tuesday of each month, they'll start anticipating its arrival.

The **Professional Look and feel** of a newsletter reflect directly on the organization. There are literally hundreds of free options to acquire professionally designed email templates—some simple, while others are quite complex. Many of them even offer plain text options allowing you to skip strict formatting while still tracking metrics and giving people the option to unsubscribe.

Show some **Personality** when writing. Let the reader get to know you. Who you are. What you believe. What's important to you? Write conversationally. Let people in on why it's so important to do the work you're doing.

> ### Did you know?
> When asked which medium people would like to receive updates from, **90%** preferred an email newsletter.

Stay **Reader-centric**. The reader must know what's being accomplished is because of their involvement and support. Focus more on using *second-person* plural pronouns such as "you" and "yours" rather than *first-person* plurals like "us" and "we." Writing in the *first-person* removes the reader from the story.

Calls to Action must be clear, concise, and obvious. Don't assume the reader will finish the newsletter and immediately draw the conclusion on what they need to do next. It won't happen. If you want the reader's opinion, ask them to take a survey. If you want them to sign up for something, ask them to do so. If you want them to click on a link, make the request. People need to be shown, guided, and steered.

Make it **Mobile-Friendly**. If the newsletter is not mobile-friendly, it may not be read by the entire audience. **54%** of smartphone owners use their devices to check their email. By 2018, the number is expected to be **80%**. **70%** of recipients delete emails immediately that don't render or display well on mobile devices. Go mobile or go home.

Always Source Your Material. It's important to credit any source used in the publication. It adds credibility and authenticity. It also avoids costly court trials and poor publicity.

Getting the newsletter into the reader's hands can take several tracks:

- The publication might reside on the website. An email is sent out with a link back to the document. This method generates more website traffic and provides users with the opportunity to explore the site.

- The publication may be attached to an email, or the newsletter may comprise the bulk of the email copy itself.

- The newsletter could be printed, distributed, or mailed to donors who do not have Internet access.

Find two Newsletter Examples at the end of this chapter.

Use whatever method works best for you and your supporters.

> **Did you know?**
> Focusing on what people receive verses what they have to do boosts the conversion rate by **44%**.
> (NextAfter.com Experiment #1621)

Don't tell people to sign up; tell them what they'll receive when they do.

Measuring Success

Once strategies are in place for the newsletter, the success rate needs to be measured and evaluated. Suppose the goal of the newsletter is to inform and educate potential supporters and donors. In that case, it will be challenging to determine if people are reading the publication unless they take some action. Action can take the form of sending an email your way, visiting the website, joining in on social media discussions, or making a gift from the donation page.

If the goal of the publication is to turn potential supporters into donors, then the only measurement we'll have is if they make a gift to the cause.

If you're trying to get the readership to act by leaving their email address, then subscriptions will be the determining factor.

If the newsletter is enclosed in an email and sent via a vehicle like Mailchimp or Constant Contact, we'll be able to tell if people received the publication and opened the message, but not whether they read what was sent. Readers will need to take some action to confirm that fact.

Google Analytics can be leveraged to track whether readers visit the website or social channels.

It's good that people are reading the newsletter and becoming informed about what the organization is accomplishing. But if the goal is to get people to engage or give, then they must take some action.

Building an Audience

There are several ways to increase your newsletter's readership. Try the ideas listed here that you believe fit your style and situation:

- **Always Mention the Fact** – Continue to find ways to raise the visibility of the newsletter. Mention it on your social media platforms or create a brief video ad for your newsletter. Add a sign-up button on your Facebook, Twitter, Pinterest, or Instagram page. Don't forget to have a prominent signup button on the website's home page. Always mention the publication when conversing with someone.

- **Create an Email Sign-up Series** – Consider creating a signup series of three or four emails highlighting what's been recently published in the newsletter.

- **Build a Home for Your Newsletters** – Consider posting your newsletters on your blog and letting people know that you're keeping the back issues available for them to access.

- **Add an Opt-in Button at the End of Each Blog Post** – Add a signup button or link at the end of each blog post.

- **Give People a Sneak Peek** – Send an email out featuring three or four of the top newsletter articles and encourage people to sign up.

- **Encourage Your Readership to Share the Publication** – Always make it easy for people to share the publication with their friends and colleagues. Don't assume people will take the time—you'll need to tell them.

- **Offer Something of Value** – If you've just written an eBook, offer it free as an incentive to sign up.

- **Make Signing Up a No-Brainer** – Ensure the signup process is straightforward and seamless. Don't ask for any information past the email address. As you build a relationship with your subscribers, you can acquire more information.

It goes without saying that the newsletter must be chock-full of value. It will be challenging to boost the readership of the publication if it's not delivering what the readers expect.

Battling Writer's Block

If you find yourself running out of writing ideas for the newsletter, refer to *Battling Blogger's Block* back in Chapter THREE.

Settling for "Good Enough"

If you find the expression "good enough" creeping into your vocabulary, perhaps think about replacing that expression with "Everything with Excellence."

Suppose you believe the newsletter is resonating with your readership. In that case, if people are saying they're enjoying the experience and engaging in two-way conversations, it's not time to take a breather, sit back, or take a break. There will always be something, or someone else, vying for your donor's attention. Keep publishing.

Work through this evaluation exercise:

<u>*Overall*</u>

- Does the newsletter provide information and resources that are not available elsewhere?

- Does the newsletter have a firm publication date, and is it sent out on time?

- Is the information in the publication "newsworthy?"

<u>*Audience*</u>

- Does the reader understand the purpose of the newsletter?

- Is the reader quickly drawn into the stories?

- Is the voice and content of the newsletter audience-appropriate?

Format

- Can the reader quickly find what interests them most?

- Does the newsletter have a professional look and feel?
- Is there a good balance of whitespace, text, and images?

- Are "attention-grabbing" headlines used to attract the reader's interest?

Content

- Does the information convey passion and excitement? Is it timely, relevant, engaging, and donor-centric?

> "**Focus more on substance and content**—than format, fonts, and colors."

- Does the depth of the content match the varied needs of the audience?

- Are there links within the text to provide resources that go beyond what's covered in the newsletter? Are there links back to the website?

- Is the content free from spelling, grammatical, and other typographical errors?

Engagement

- Are people writing back? Is there a means to make that happen?

- Are readers making their way to the website or social platforms? Are they being encouraged to do so?

Reach

- Can readers easily share the newsletter?

- Are you acquiring new email addresses from people outside your sphere of influence?

Remember to seek the advice and counsel of a few trusted associates. The more familiar they are with writing or publishing, the better. There's not much to be gained from someone who does not write themselves.

Perhaps, a conversation with several of the more avid readers could shed light on how the newsletter might be enhanced or improved.

The Pros and Cons

With the good may come the not-so-good. Newsletters are a great form of communication, but their publication can take a toll on your resources. Look at the list of pluses and minuses before taking on an added endeavor of this sort.

Pros and Cons of Newsletters	
Pros	**Cons**
• Increases retention	• Can be time consuming
• Boosts loyalty	• Can be resource draining
• Regular contact	• Publishing deadlines
• Builds community	• Limited space
• Easy to deliver	• Fresh material
• Inexpensive	• Newsworthy
• Easy to start	• Hard to keep going
• Results can be measured	• Reader expectations

Several statistics in this chapter courtesy of: Statistics that Prove Email Marketing is (Still) Not Dead, posted by Caroline Malamut on February 4, 2016.

SHOW & TELL

Newsletter
Example (1)

Download at:

johndleavy.com/PC/NewsletterExample.pdf

SHOW & TELL

Newsletter Promotional Email Example

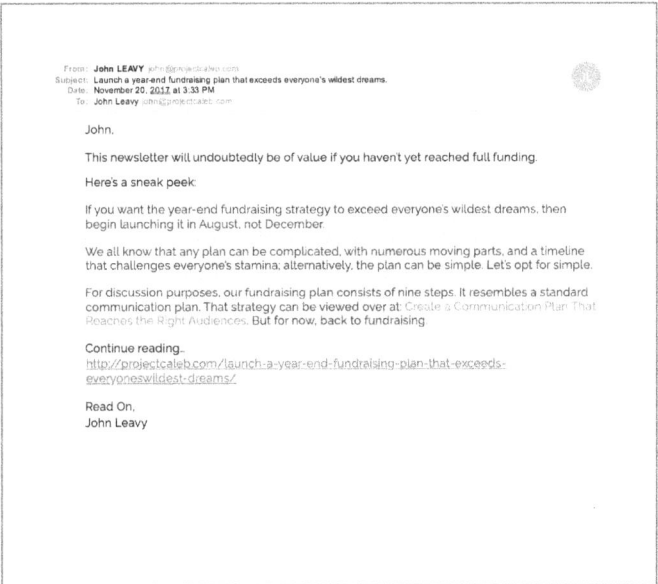

From: **John LEAVY** john@projectcaleb.com
Subject: Launch a year-end fundraising plan that exceeds everyone's wildest dreams.
Date: November 20, 2017 at 3:33 PM
To: **John Leavy** john@projectcaleb.com

John,

This newsletter will undoubtedly be of value if you haven't yet reached full funding.

Here's a sneak peek:

If you want the year-end fundraising strategy to exceed everyone's wildest dreams, then begin launching it in August, not December.

We all know that any plan can be complicated, with numerous moving parts, and a timeline that challenges everyone's stamina; alternatively, the plan can be simple. Let's opt for simple.

For discussion purposes, our fundraising plan consists of nine steps. It resembles a standard communication plan. That strategy can be viewed over at: Create a Communication Plan That Reaches the Right Audiences. But for now, back to fundraising.

Continue reading...
http://projectcaleb.com/launch-a-year-end-fundraising-plan-that-exceeds-everyoneswildest-dreams/

Read On,
John Leavy

Download at:

johndleavy.com/PC/NewsletterPromotionalEmailExample.pdf

SIX

Create **AMAZING**
Appeal Letters

A ppeal letters can have several objectives. The letter could be an appeal for an end-of-the-year gift, for monthly financial support, or to fund a special project. Newsletters sent out monthly or email updates that have a link at the end of the message, inferring the recipient should visit the organization's donation page, are not effective appeal letters.

In some instances, an appeal letter may be sent soliciting volunteers, needed supplies, or resources.

Appeal letters have a definite, understood purpose by both parties. The organization is seeking help or assistance of some kind.

Appeal letters are all about the donor, not the organization.

Appeal letters should differ from every other communication the donor receives from the organization.

In the Appeal Letter Example that follows, constituents are asked to support Project:Caleb financially for the speaking opportunity at the June 2018 Association of Gospel Rescue Missions Conference in Milwaukee, Wisconsin.

Anatomy of an Appeal Letter

⑤ The Association of Gospel Rescue Missions (AGRM) has already extended an invitation for us to speak at their national gathering in 2018.

Being able to pay for the trip will be challenging. Project:Caleb has not appealed for support in the past, but perhaps God has other plans.

Here's what the trip will cost:

⑥
- Join AGRM's Business Partners – $440/annual fee
- Airfare – $382 (of course this changes minute-by-minute)
- Hotel – $129 per night for four nights
- Conference registration – $489 (early-bird registration ends 12/15)

The total cost is $1,827. Would you consider sponsoring a portion of this trip or perhaps a single item such as the plane fare or conference fee?

⑦ Like King David when raising funds for building the temple, I have donated the first $200.

Coming along side this venture, be blessed, and bless others?

⑧ Donations can be made online at joytotheworld.org. Just search for Project Caleb and click the "DONATE NOW TO THIS PROJECT" button on our donation page. This is a tax-deductible donation.

Be in prayer as God works this out.

⑨ Can't wait to share the exciting details of the Milwaukee trip after attending.

Look to Him.
John

1. **Heading** – Let's assume we all know to start the communique out with the company logo, contact information, current date, and a personalized salutation.

2. **Tag line** – Think about including a statistic to add authority and legitimacy to the needed-support argument as a regular staple of our appeal letters. Here's what we said: ***Did you know that 50% of ministries and non-profits never raise more than $10,000? 82% fail to***

raise their first $100,000. Statistics help people understand the urgency and magnitude of the problem. The recipients also become aware that the organization is on top of the situation—connected, they know what's happening.

3. **Opening Sentences** – The opening sentences should set the stage for the discussion. It should explain the problem and talk about the organization's solution.

4. **Add Authority** – It's always beneficial to incorporate an authoritative voice or two to support the organization's approach in resolving the problem. Here, two testimonial quotes are added.

5. **People Need Deadlines** – People need to know when things are happening. In this case, the first conference speaking opportunity will take place from June 15 to 18, 2018.

6. **The Funds Necessary** – It's essential to provide donors with the details on the amount required and how the funds will be allocated. In this example, the membership fee, airfare, hotel, and conference fee are itemized.

7. **Biblical Support** – it never hurts to refer to the most authoritative source on this planet. Here, King David's

financial support for building God's temple is mentioned. Project:Caleb is also noting that the project's founder is donating the first $200. Are the leadership and advisory board members financially supporting the organization's efforts?

8. **How to Donate** – If the person receiving the appeal letter is to act, they must be instructed to do so. The gifting process must be obvious, secure, and flawless.

9. **Closing** – The closing should thank the person in advance for their time and consideration. Make it personal. Its appeal needs to come from a real person.

Developing an Appeal Letter Strategy

Don't lose sight of the fact that the appeal letter's first objective is to either foster a burgeoning relationship with the potential supporter or to build on one that's already been cultivated.

Get in the habit of using the words "you" and "yours" more than "we" and "us." Words such as "you" immediately bring the reader into the story.

Focus on impact. How are people's lives being changed? How is the problem getting better? What life's challenges existed before that do not exist now?

How are the funds being allocated? People must know their money is being spent wisely.

Find an Appeal Letter Example at the end of this chapter.

Stick to one concern in the letter. Don't use it as a catch-all for everything the organization wants to do over the next few years.

Show passion.

Use POWERFUL words.

Give the donor a deadline. When is the money needed? Give the person options on how they might contribute. Break the need down into amounts people can understand. It's challenging for a person to grasp numbers such as $75,000, $300,000, or $2.5 million.

Converting Recipients into Donors

A significant number of people who receive their first appeal letter will not be ready to decide.

> **Did you know?**
> **95%** to **97%** of people arriving at a website are not ready to make a decision.

What is an organization to do?

The only choice is to help that person decide.

How does that happen?

By engaging, educating, and nurturing each relationship. Through that process, the potential donor will hopefully gain the necessary information needed to decide if they want to be involved or support the work financially.

- No matter what the objective of the appeal letter is, it must always deliver value.

- Tell stories that are compelling, relevant, timely, interesting, donor-centric, and sprinkled with empathy and emotion.

- Offer something for the reader's time and consideration— perhaps a free eBook.

- Create a campaign of three to four emails that educate potential donors about the obstacles facing the organization and the people it serves.

- Create an instant response mechanism to ensure questions are answered promptly.

- Collect as much information as possible about potential donors. Get to know them. What is it that they are passionate about? What do they want to see accomplished?

- Make sure every piece of material sent their way creates a positive experience.

- Last, use a combination of hard and soft "asks." Provide potential supporters with opportunities to participate beyond giving.

Measuring Success

If appeal letters are mailed via the US Mail, the only way to measure success will be when people visit the donation page and click the DONATE button.

If the letters are sent via an email system such as Mailchimp, more metrics can be tracked. We'll know how many people opened the support letter email, clicked on the donation page, and then gave a gift.

The nurturing process that's put in place also tells how well *that* strategy is working.

If the appeal letter is not yielding positive results, consider adjusting it. Try different openings, various stories, diverse calls–to-action.

The results won't change unless your actions do.

Settling for "Good Enough"

There's always room for improvement. Let the expression "Everything with Excellence" permeate your thought process when looking for ways to improve the results, no matter how positive.

Work through this evaluation exercise:

<u>Overall</u>

- Have the right potential supporters been identified?

- Has the purpose of the letter been well thought out?

- Does the letter take the reader through a logical progression of the problem and the organization's solution?

Audience

- Does the reader understand the purpose of the letter?

- Does the reader understand the urgency?

- Does the reader feel they can be a part of the solution?

- Does the appeal/solution make sense to the reader?

Format

- Does the letter have a professional look and feel?

- Is there a good balance of whitespace, text, and images?

- Was an attention-grabbing headline used?

- Is the letter more than one page? (More than one page for a solid reason?)

Content

- Does the information convey passion and excitement? Is it timely, relevant, interesting, and donor-centric?

- Is the need clearly explained and justified?
- Are the supportive details included?

- Is the content free from spelling, grammatical, and other typographical errors?

- Have any authoritative voices been added?

Engagement

- Is there a mechanism for people to ask questions?

- Are the recipients encouraged to engage?

- Is the donation process secure and trouble-free?

Reach

- Can the reader easily share the appeal letter with family and friends?

- Are you acquiring information on new potential contacts?

Remember to seek the advice and counsel of a few trusted donors. It's always good to get another perspective.

The Pros and Cons

This list of pros and cons helps you understand the commitment involved in sending out appeal letters.

Pros and Cons of Appeal Letters	
Pros	**Cons**
• Increases retention	• Can be time consuming
• Boosts donor loyalty	• Writing challenge
• Regular contact	• Missed deadlines
• Builds engagement	• Ineffective ask
• Easy to deliver	• Fresh material
• Inexpensive	• Not impactful
• Easy to start	• Hard to keep going
• Results can be measured	• Missed expectations

Appeal Letter Example (1)

Download at:

johndleavy.com/PC/AppealLetterExample.pdf

SEVEN

(10 MIN READ)

Create **AMAZING** Brochures

Brochures serve several purposes. The publication can showcase an organization's work on specific projects in a remote area of a foreign country, or it can discuss the organization's vision, mission, and purpose. They can be printed and sent to potential supporters and donors via the US Mail, or they may be transmitted electronically via email.

Brochures can serve as "leave-behinds" at the end of face-to-face meetings with potential donors.

Did you know?
75% of the people in a recent survey considered brochures to be a useful information resource.

Anatomy of an AMAZING Brochure

Here are two tri-fold brochure examples:

③

The AGMT prepares pastors, plants churches, and provides educational opportunities in every country starting in West Africa and crossing the continent to the East. Under the direction of the Cross Ministries International this project has ministries in Ghana, Togo, and Benin. In its 15-year history, the project has planted churches, provided relief for struggling communities, trained and supported pastors, built a school, and raised support for various health missions.

"As you go, preach, saying, 'The Kingdom of heaven is at hand.' Heal the sick, cleanse the lepers, raise the dead, cast out demons. Freely you have received, freely give."
Matthew 10:7&8

Join us now.
www.africangospelmega-transect.org

②

The AGMT's mission is to make Christ known; we will accomplish this by "multiplying ministry throughout Africa." We are racing against time; the challenges of Africa, false teachings, and spiritual forces of darkness in reaching the millions of Africans with the hope of the Gospel of the Finished Work. Jesus said,

"The Harvest is plentiful but the laborers are few. Pray to the Lord of the Harvest that He might send laborers into the fields."

The Harvest is now. The AGMT needs laborers and people who are willing to invest in the harvest. You may not be called to go forth into this field as a "going missionary," but you can be a "giving missionary" involved in the Harvest.
www.africangospelmega-transect.org

African Gospel Mega-Transect

(417) 741-6773
joe@africangospelmega-transect.org

①

AFRICAN GOSPEL MEGA-TRANSECT

⑥ Providing Educational Opportunities

African families struggle to provide their children with basic educational experiences. Families cannot afford tuition.

Children are left behind.

The AGMT is looking to create schools within local churches linking the churches to the community to help advance the next generation. The schools would provide hot meals to these students, many of which would not get a nutritious meal if it were not for this lunch.

You can join us in this project by donating to:

www.africangospelmega-transect.org

⑤ Planting Churches

Jesus told His disciples they would be His witnesses to the "uttermost parts of the world." The village of Esumankrom in Ghana's Western Region has no church, no Gospel being proclaimed.

The AGMT is committed to plant Gospel proclaiming churches.

Church plants, like the new church in Ekon, Ghana, need places of worship, instruments, sound systems, chairs, and bibles. The people live in depressed areas and cannot provide the church's basic needs. Many are unable to support their pastors.

④ Preparing Pastors

The goal of AGMT is to Prepare Pastors throughout Africa in the accuracy of the Gospel.

How to disciple members, shepherding the congregation, and to supply them with resources and support in their work. Training Centers will be created so pastors can attend 6 week to 3 month vigorous courses that will better prepare them for their work. Many pastors cannot afford the training cost; we need partners to make this possible.

In examining the six panels of the first brochure, we notice:

Panel 1 – The first panel includes the organization's logo and a photo of the area in Africa where they minister.

Panel 2 – The second panel discusses AGMT's mission, the urgent need for support, the organization's website, and it's contact information.

Panel 3 – The third panel discusses AGMT's overall objectives.

Panels 4, 5, 6 – Panels four, five, and six highlight the projects AGMT uses to accomplish their mission: providing for orphan children, church planting, and teaching pastors about the accuracy of the Bible.

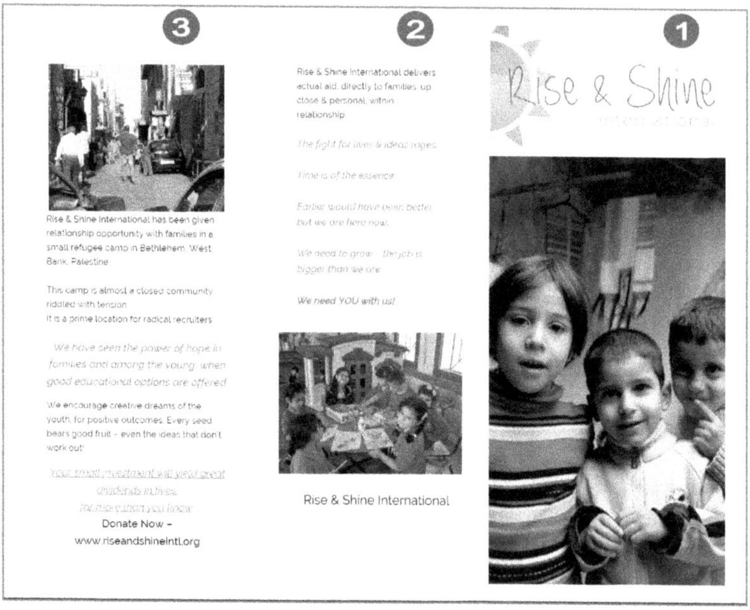

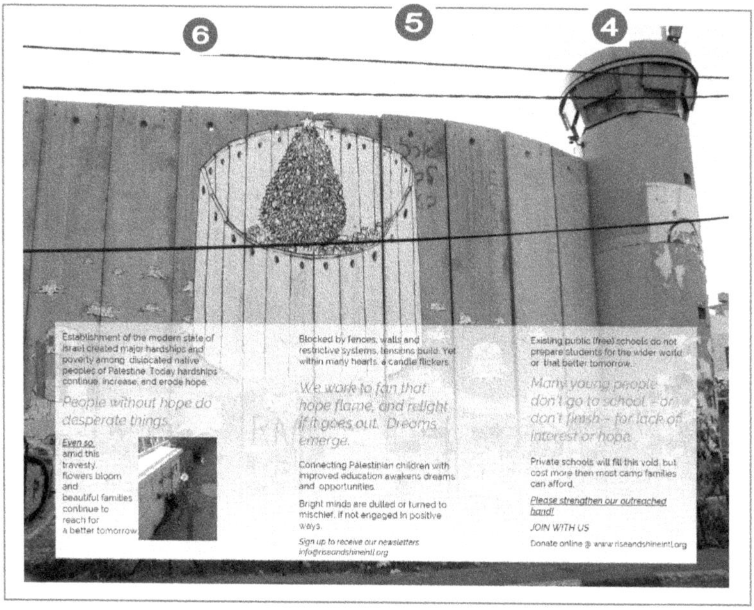

In the second brochure's six panels, we observe:

Panel 1 – The first panel features the organization's logo and an engaging photo of school children in the area where they minister.

Panel 2 – The second panel discusses R&S's mission, features a strong call to action, and includes a photo of the school children.

Panel 3 – The third panel discusses R&S's focus on the conditions under which they work, along with another plea, and the website.

Panels 4, 5, 6 – Panels four, five, and six feature a powerful image in the background, along with more information on R&S objectives, facts about the educational programs they offer, and their email address and website.

SHOW & TELL **Find two Brochure Examples at the end of this chapter. Please do not plagiarize this content.**

Developing a Brochure Strategy

When developing a brochure strategy, it is a good practice to have both a high-resolution version for printing and a low-resolution version for emailing to potential supporters and donors.

A brochure strategy might include three objectives: first, as an introduction piece when meeting with potential new donors. The publication could feature the organization's vision, mission, and purpose. A second brochure might discuss the various projects or work currently underway. A third brochure version might be used to discuss a specific project, planned event, or end-of-year fundraising effort.

There are brochure templates galore on the Internet but consider using a professional to design and build the piece. The extra time, effort, and expense necessary will be invaluable.

Measuring Success

Measuring the success of brochures, whether mailed out, or handed out will be difficult unless they prompt the recipients to take some action—such as subscribing to your newsletter, visiting your website, or making a donation.

If brochures are sent out via email, consider using an automated marketing system such as Mailchimp or Constant Contact. At least, the email opens can be tracked. If the electronic brochure includes links, click-throughs can also be tallied.

In one sense, a person can tell if the brochure is doing its job by the fact that people receiving it have fewer questions about the organization.

Make the brochure a keeper!

Settling for "Good Enough"

It's time for our "Good Enough" section again. Are you still thinking of "Everything with Excellence?"

When considering creating a brochure, remember that it adds credibility to the organization, provides people with a tangible reminder of the organization, and keeps the organization's needs front and center.

> **Did you know?**
> **70%** of Americans prefer to read on paper and **67%** prefer printed materials over digital.

It's time for our evaluation exercise:

Overall

- Are the goals for the brochure well defined?

- Has the target audience for the brochure been decided?

- Has its delivery method been settled?

- Is it obvious what people should do after reading the brochure?

Audience

- Does the reader understand the purpose of the brochure?

- Are there audience/project reasons to have more than one brochure?

- Is the voice and content of the brochure audience-appropriate?

Format

- Does the brochure information have a logical flow?

- Does the brochure have a professional look and feel?

- Is there a good balance of whitespace, text, and images?

- Are "attention-grabbing" headlines used to attract the reader's interest?

Content

- Does the information convey passion and excitement? Is it

*"**Focus more on substance and content**—than format, fonts, and colors."*

timely, relevant, engaging, and donor-centric?

- Does the content tell a compelling story?

- Are the contact information and website name obvious?

- Is the content free from spelling, grammatical, and other typographical errors?

Engagement

- Does the brochure include an information panel, and are people filling out the card? Are they mailing it?

- Are readers making their way to the website or social platforms? Are they being encouraged to do so?

Reach

- Have you considered providing people with more than one brochure so they can easily share the information with a friend?

- Is the brochure helping you acquire new email addresses from people outside your sphere of influence?

Remember to bring a few trusted friends into the discussion when developing the brochure's look as well as its content. The more familiar they are with writing or publishing, the better.

The Pros and Cons

Examining the pros and cons of a new undertaking is always helpful. Review the list of pluses and minuses.

Pros and Cons of Brochures	
Pros	**Cons**
• Low cost if sent electronically	• Limited reach
• Flexibility	• May minimize creativity
• Portability	• Needs to be professionally done
• Good introduction piece	• Print and mailing costs
• Easy to hand out	• Risks Obsolesces
• Good first impression	• May not be the right communication vehicle
• Adds legitimacy to the organization	• Unable to measure its effect

Statistic in this chapter courtesy of a 2010 study by Bentley University professor Ian Cross.

Statistic in this chapter courtesy of a European survey of interviewed consumers of 13 countries where print users who use digital media with certain regularity.

AGMT Brochure Example

Download at:

johndleavy.com/PC/AGMTBrochureExample.pdf

R&S Brochure Example

Download at:

johndleavy.com/PC/RandSBrochureExample.pdf

EIGHT

Create **AMAZING** Presentations

T here are three main ingredients in any presentation: the slides, the material covered during the talk, and the presenter. These factors must be congruent, or the presentation may not yield the desired results.

In *Create **AMAZING** Presentations*, let's examine each element to understand what it takes to pull off a successful presentation, whether to one individual or a small group.

The slides need to look professional. Think crisp and clear and not overloaded with text and images. Less is more. The conversation should be on point, fast-paced, and passionate. The presenter must be engaging, maintain good eye contact, and deliver a convincing presentation, prompting people to act.

Anatomy of an AMAZING Presentation

The Slides

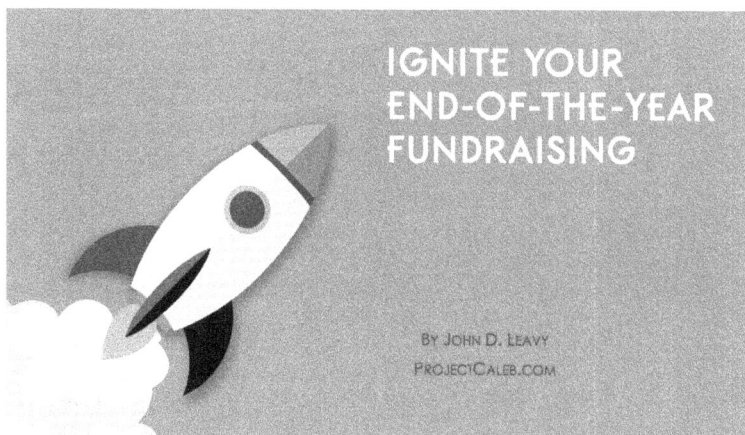

The slides need to be clear, concise, and easy to read. The colors should be coordinated and pleasing to the eye. The slides should not be crammed with text and images. Less is always better. Leave open space on each slide.

Ensure the colors work well when projected on a large screen. Stick with colors that do not fade when highlighted.

The Material Covered

Limit the number of slides to tell the story—10 to 12 slides should do the trick. The presentation should last between 10 and 15 minutes. Here's a potential example:

Slide 0 – Title slide

Slide 1 – State the problem and its potential impact

Slide 2 – Ministry or project overview

Slide 3 – Introduce the services or products you would provide a cure for the problem

Slide 4 – Talk about organization, execution, and cost

Slide 5 – Talk about how the project would evolve

Slide 6 – Talk about any progress made so far

Slide 7 – Talk about the management and advisory team

Slide 8 – Talk about how the plan might be scaled up if funds were available

Slide 9 – Talk about the finances

Slide 10 – Talk about the challenges/risks

Slide 11 – Talk about how one might be involved

Slide 12 – Thank you

SHOW & TELL **Find Presentation Slide Examples and Worksheet at the end of this chapter.**

The slides should evoke emotion and contribute to the story being told. Consider dimming the photo (increasing the transparency) in the background so the text on top is more readable.

The red text along the bottom of the slide serves as a reference and for copyright protection. Notice how it does not attract a person's eye.

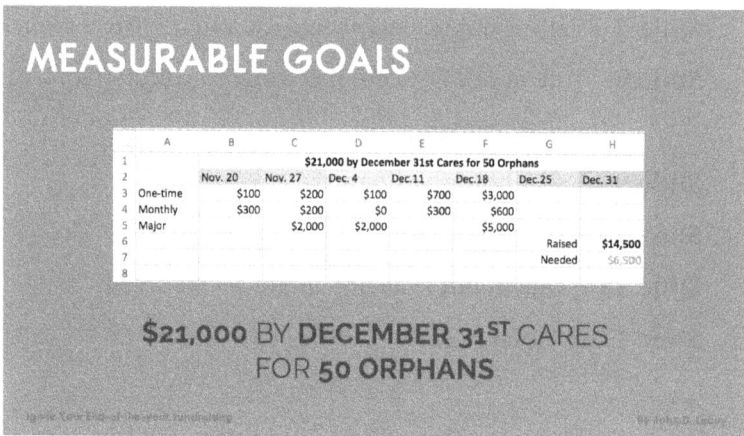

Every illustration on the slides needs to be readable. It makes little sense to show photos or illustrations that people cannot make out and then proceed to tell them what they cannot see.

Go easy on the effects, transitions, music, and sounds. That technology adds little to the message and only distracts the viewer. The observer will spend more time listening to the sounds or watching the elements fly around on the screen rather than paying attention to what the presenter is saying.

The Presenter

It's up to the presenter to keep the presentation interesting. Keep the conversation brief. Keep things moving. Don't bore the person listening.

Practice, practice, practice.

Don't read the slides. The slides are just conversation starters, not the focus.

Here's a list of common mistakes made by presenters:

- Lack of understanding of who the audience is
- Choosing a poor meeting space
- Stiffness
- Distracting body language
- Poor eye contact
- The speaker seems uncomfortable
- Rambles at times
- Lacks excitement, enthusiasm, or passion
- Inability to listen
- Not familiar with the technology being used
- Not being clear and to the point
- Boring slide headlines and images
- Poor preparation
- Droning on and on

Developing a Presentation Strategy

What does one hope to accomplish in doing the presentation? Is the goal to raise the organization's visibility, recruit volunteers, showcase progress on ongoing projects, or raise funds?

First, determine the objective(s) of the presentation and decide how success will be measured. Then, start laying out the slide format and outline.

Here are a series of questions to consider when developing your strategy before building the presentation:

Who will put the slides together? – Will this be the job for one person, or is a writer or graphic artist available?

Find a Presentation Slides Worksheet at the end of this chapter.

Have the audiences been identified? – It's important to talk about what matters most to the one listening, not the one presenting.

Have other presentations been acquired? – Don't reinvent the wheel. Learn from other people's successes. *We're not suggesting plagiarism be employed.* But look around and see what example presentations you might learn from.

How will the presentation be managed? – The information in the presentation obviously needs to stay current. Who will take on that assignment?

Will the presentation slides be transmitted? – Some think it's a good idea to email the slide presentation to the one who listened after the fact. Others think the slides are of little use without the presenter. If the slides are not self-explanatory, skip the email option.

Measuring Success

It will be challenging to measure the presentation's success unless the objectives are clearly defined and measurable.

Are more people becoming aware of the organization? Perhaps the number of website visits or social media connections is increasing, or volunteers are stepping up following a recent presentation. Are potential supporters and donors more educated about the progress being made on projects in the field? Has there been an increase in gift-giving?

Settling for "Good Enough"

Let's cover "Good Enough" once more.

Presentations may inform or educate, inspire or motivate, activate or stimulate. Try not to do everything at once. Presentations can be a powerful tool for conveying your message.

Here's an evaluation exercise to peruse:

Overall

- Are the presentation goals well-defined and measurable?

- Has the target audience for the presentation been decided?

- Has professional help been sought in the design?

- What should people do after hearing the presentation?

Audience

- Is the purpose of the presentation apparent to those listening?

- Are there audience/project reasons to have more than one presentation?

- Is the voice and content of the presentation audience-appropriate?

Format

- Does the presentation have a professional look and feel?

- Is there a good balance of whitespace, text, and images?

- Are "attention-grabbing" headlines used to keep the reader's interest?

- Is the presentation limited to 10 - 12 slides?

- Does the presentation show well when projected?

Content

- Does the information convey passion and excitement? Is it timely, relevant, engaging, and donor-centric?

- Is the story compelling?

- Is there a good, logical flow to the material presented?

- Is the content free from spelling, grammatical, and other typographical errors?

Engagement

- Does the presentation pique the listener's interest?

- Are those listening responding positively?

- Are they being encouraged to connect to the organization to find out more?

- Are all their questions being answered?

Reach

- Is the presentation helping you acquire new potential contacts?

- Is the presentation showcased on your social channels?

- Are you seeking feedback?

- Have you considered posting individual slides on your social channels?

The Pros and Cons

Examining the pros and cons of a new undertaking is always helpful. Review the list of pluses and minuses.

Pros and Cons of Presentations	
Pros	**Cons**
• Use anywhere	• Slide overkill
• More interesting	• Speaking can be stressful
• Individuality	• Fear
• Affordable	• Time mismanagement
• Professional looking	• Lack of control
• Allows for collaboration	• Difficult to measure
• Easy learning style	• Missed expectations
• Concise message	

SHOW & TELL

Presentation Slides
Example (1)

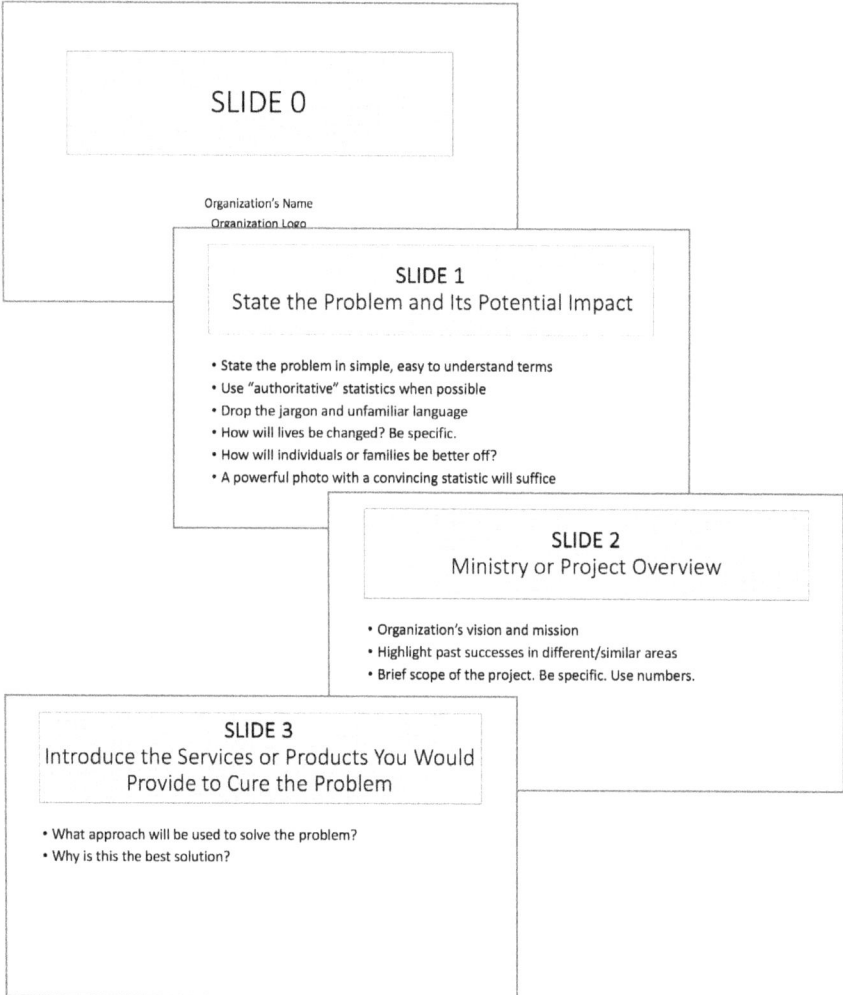

SLIDE 0

Organization's Name
Organization Logo

SLIDE 1
State the Problem and Its Potential Impact

- State the problem in simple, easy to understand terms
- Use "authoritative" statistics when possible
- Drop the jargon and unfamiliar language
- How will lives be changed? Be specific.
- How will individuals or families be better off?
- A powerful photo with a convincing statistic will suffice

SLIDE 2
Ministry or Project Overview

- Organization's vision and mission
- Highlight past successes in different/similar areas
- Brief scope of the project. Be specific. Use numbers.

SLIDE 3
Introduce the Services or Products You Would
Provide to Cure the Problem

- What approach will be used to solve the problem?
- Why is this the best solution?

Download at:

johndleavy.com/PC/PresentationSlidesExample.pptx

SHOW & TELL

Presentation Slides Example (2)

SLIDE 4
Talk About Organization, Execution, and Cost

- Organizational successes in this area
- Highlight team's experience
- Outline project cost

SLIDE 5
Talk About How the Project Would Evolve

- Take those through the execution steps from beginning to end
- Use a timeline. There must be a deadline.

SLIDE 6
Talk About Any Progress Made So Far

- If the project has not begun, drop this slide
- Talk about the progress made, the obstacles overcome, and how things are getting better for those receiving the aid

SLIDE 7
Talk About the Management and Advisory Team

- Talk about how the project will be managed
- Showcase the skills of those involved

Download at:

johndleavy.com/PC/PresentationSlidesExample.pptx

SHOW & TELL

Presentation Slides
Example (3)

SLIDE 8
Talk About How the Plan Might Be Scaled If
More Funds Were Made Available

• If more funds were made available what's the vision past this project?

SLIDE 9
Talk About the Financials

• Talk about how the fund would come in
• How would they be expended?
• How would expenses be approved and tracked?

SLIDE 10
Talk About the Challenges/Risks

• Are there local challenges or risks?
• Is there the possibility of government interference?
• How do the nationals feel about the project?
• How will these types of challenges/risks be overcome?

SLIDE 11
Talk About How One Might Be Involved

• How might those listening be involved? Be specific? Give deadlines?
• Are there ways to be involved beyond financial giving?

Download at:

johndleavy.com/PC/PresentationSlidesExample.pptx

SHOW &TELL

Presentation Slides
Example (4)

SLIDE 12
Thank you

- Thank people for their time
- Be gracious
- End things believing God will provide

Download at:

johndleavy.com/PC/PresentationSlidesExample.pptx

SHOW & TELL

Presentation Slides
Worksheet (1)

Presentation Slides
Worksheet

Use this worksheet to develop the slide presentation content. The blank lines are provided for the messaging. Think about the images or photos that would be included.

1. **Slide 0** – Title slide

_____

☐ Illustration?   ☐ Photo?

2. **Slide 1** – State the problem and its potential impact.

_____

☐ Illustration?   ☐ Photo?

3. **Slide 2** – Ministry or project overview.

_____

☐ Illustration?   ☐ Photo?

4. **Slide 3** – Introduce the services or products you would provide to cure the problem.

_____

☐ Illustration?   ☐ Photo?

5. **Slide 4** – Talk about organization, execution, and cost.

_____

☐ Illustration?   ☐ Photo?

Copyright © 2018 Project.Caleb

Download at:

johndleavy.com/PC/PresentationSlidesWorksheet.pdf

Presentation Slides
Worksheet (2)

6. **Slide 5** – Talk about the project would evolve.

_____

☐ Illustration?   ☐ Photo?

7. **Slide 6** – Talk about progress so far.

_____

☐ Illustration?   ☐ Photo?

8. **Slide 7** – Talk about the management and advisory team.

_____

☐ Illustration?   ☐ Photo?

9. **Slide 8** – Talk about how the plan might be scaled up if funds were available.

_____

☐ Illustration?   ☐ Photo?

10. **Slide 9** – Talk about then financial challenges.

_____

☐ Illustration?   ☐ Photo?

11. **Slide 10** – Talk about the challenges/risks.

_____

☐ Illustration?   ☐ Photo?

Copyright © 2018 Project:Caleb

Download at:

johndleavy.com/PC/PresentationSlidesWorksheet.docx

SHOW &TELL

Presentation Slides
Worksheet (3)

---

12. Slide 11 – Talk about how one might be involved

_____

☐ Illustration?   ☐ Photo?

13. Slide 12 – Talk about how one might be involved

_____

☐ Illustration?   ☐ Photo?

Copyright © 2018 Project Caleb

Download at:

johndleavy.com/PC/PresentationSlidesWorksheet.pdf

NINE

(14 MIN READ)

Create **AMAZING**
Face-to-face Meetings

[Portions of this chapter are excerpted from Ignite Your End-of-the-year Fundraising, the first book in the Ignition Series.]

Productive face-to-face meetings do not happen without planning, preparation, practice, and prayer. The Sage Exchange in the UK lists five crucial advantages of face-to-face meetings:

> ### Did you know?
> The yes-rate for face-to-face appeals around the world with those trained in face-to-face appeals is **50-70%**? (Blind Spots by Scott Morton)

1. **Body language** – most communication is transmitted through people's body language, hand gestures, and facial expressions. The opportunity to *read* people is invaluable.

2. **Donors appreciate it** – people will appreciate the fact that you're taking the time to meet with them personally.

The face-to-face also allows you the opportunity to make a favorable impression.

3. **Deeper insights** – The location of the meeting may seem unimportant, but it reveals a great deal about the person who chose the place. Is it noisy? Confusing? Inappropriate? If the meeting takes place at the organization's headquarters, is the office disorganized and cluttered?

4. **Get to know the inside story** – Face-to-face meetings lend themselves to being more informal. It puts both parties at ease.

5. **Develop transparency and trust** – Face-to-face meetings cultivate trust. These types of meetings are integral to building a solid relationship.

Anatomy of an AMAZING Face-to-face Meeting

Productive face-to-face meetings rarely happen by chance—they're planned. Here's how a typical scenario might go:

1. A potential supporter is identified
2. A call or email is initiated to set a time aside to meet
3. The get-together takes place
4. Follow-up happens

Developing a Face-to-face Strategy

The first task is to create a list of potential people to contact for a face-to-face. If you're having trouble coming up with the names of people to contact, here are some ideas to get you started on making a list:

- Family and friends
- Your acquaintances at church (past churches?)
- Those from small groups you've attended
- Neighbors (past neighbors?)
- Those you work with (past business associates?)
- Friends from college
- Friends from social, civic, or professional organizations
- Professionals that cross your path (doctors, lawyers, accountants, teachers)
- Contractors (plumbers, heating & air conditioning specialists, landscapers, handymen)

You'll need to work on your list over several days or perhaps a few weeks. Keep revisiting the list as names come to mind.

Find a Potential Contacts Worksheet at the end of this chapter.

As you build your list, decide what information you'd like to gather about each prospective donor. Initially, their name, email address, and phone number may be sufficient for verification purposes.

Later, you'll want to start classifying people based on how they respond, their interests in the projects you have going, and how and when they donate.

Don't ask people for more personal information than you initially plan to use. It's only natural for individuals to think they'll receive something in the mail if they provide their street address.

70% of Americans give to charitable organizations. People who give, give, and people who don't, don't. The number one indicator of a person offering to your organization is that they're already giving elsewhere.

Don't wait to start setting appointments until you have exhausted every possible person you can think of—that practice may be akin to procrastination. The sooner you begin setting appointments, the more at ease you'll be with the process going forward, and the sooner you'll be on your way to raising the funds needed by your organization.

Now that you have your list, let's discuss calling for an appointment.

Calling for an appointment

First, you'll have to set an appointment to meet with the person. Second, during that initial meeting, you'll want to share what God's doing and your story—the passion of why you do what you do. This is not the time to ask them to donate—that comes later.

The goal of the first meeting is really to set a second time to talk.

Once the person understands the organization's mission and you've shared your passion, they will want to go home, discuss it with their spouse, consider getting involved in whatever way, and ask God how they should proceed.

Think about walking onto a car lot. You don't point to the first car you see and tell the salesperson, "I'll take that one." You ask questions, kick the tires, open the hood, take it for a test drive, and perhaps even go home and think long and hard about the purchase and the financing. People donating to a cause are not much different.

Remember, the question uppermost in every potential donor's mind when you first meet will be, "***Why should I give to this organization instead of another worthwhile cause?***"

Focus on **why** you're doing what you do, not what, **how,** and **when**. Yes, it's good to tell people you're involved in building a medical clinic in a small, out-of-the-way village in Congo. Yes, it's important to inform potential donors about the care it provides to the locals once it is operational. And it's even relevant to say to them when the work will be completed.

But, it's most important for people to know "**why**" you're doing what you're doing. The clinic will improve people's lives. There will be fewer diseases. Healthier birth rates. Longer lifespans. Less suffering. A better quality of life all around.

Once they understand your mission and hear your passion, they can make the best decision about or whether they should be involved.

Provide people with various ways to get involved. Perhaps they can join the advisory team, volunteer, or

share their talents or gifts at some point. Fundraising is not always about the money.

Setting an Appointment

You'll need a script to ensure you cover everything that needs to be said when making the appointment phone calls.

Your script does not have to be a word-for-word speech—it's a quick reference guide in case you get lost or to keep you from forgetting what to say.

Find an Appointment Setting Script Example and Worksheet at the end of this chapter.

Remember, the goal of this first call is to gain an opportunity to meet with the person.

Have a backup plan if people do not have time to talk or if they say "no" to the meeting.

If the person says it's not a convenient time to talk, ask if you can call at a more convenient time. Be specific…Tuesday evening is better…next week, Wednesday?

If the person says it's not a good time to meet, ask if you can send them information about the organization, and then follow up to answer any questions they may have.

Focus on telling people where your heart is. This is an opportunity to work where God is doing great things. It's not always about giving money to the cause.

Find Information and Donor Card Examples at the end of this chapter.

So, let's say you land your first appointment. Now what?

Your First Face-to-face Meeting

Get organized before the meeting. Ensure you have the items you'd like to share, such as a business card, brochure, or video, whatever.

You'll need a second script when you do meet with people. It serves the same purpose as the one used for setting your appointments—it keeps you on track and ensures that all necessary topics are discussed.

Find a Face-to-face Meeting Script Example and Worksheet at the end of this chapter.

Run through of the conversation script in your hand; and if a trusted colleague can listen to your presentation, all the better. The more often you practice your delivery, the more comfortable and confident you'll become.

Here are five reasons why Craig Jarrow, the Time Management Ninja, believes face-to-face meetings—Get it done:

1. Body language plays a significant role in how we communicate with people
2. Ensures engagement
3. Helps clarify things—it's hard to raise your hand while on the phone
4. Drives participation
5. Tends to be more efficient

You'll obviously be able to see the other person's reaction as well as measure their interest level in what you say during your time together.

Measuring Success

In one sense, the effectiveness of some of the face-to-face meetings will be apparent. The person being presented with the challenge decides to support the organization's efforts.

Many of the other discussions will require follow-up over subsequent days and weeks. Some meeting conclusions may never be apparent.

It will be important to track the metrics that tell the story:

- How many calls were made?
- How many contacts were reached?
- How many meetings were scheduled?
- How many meetings took place?
- How many contacts said, "yes"
- How many contacts said, "no"?
- How many had to be followed up on?
- How many follow-ups produced positive results?
- How many follow-ups ended with negative results?

Gathering feedback from every meeting will be invaluable in helping to improve the success rate of the face-to-face meetings.

Settling for "Good Enough"

Let's cover "Good Enough" once again.

Face-to-face meetings are by far the most productive for mining new contacts. Make sure you do the due diligence necessary before the get-together. Listen more than talk, show passion, tell a great story, and give the person options on how they might be involved.

Here's an evaluation exercise to peruse:

Overall

- Are the goals for face-to-face interactions well-defined and measurable?

- Was there a clear resolution to the meeting?

- Do both parties understand the steps and their respective responsibilities?

- Was the time together informative and engaging?

Audience

- Is the purpose of the face-to-face meeting apparent to those invited?

- Were you conscious of the body language being displayed?

- Was the location workable?

- Was there a good balance of conversation between both parties?

Format

- Were the handouts perceived as having a professional look and feel?

- Was the format beneficial?

- Are there ways to improve the meeting?

Content

- Was the information conveyed with passion and excitement?

- Did the slides or brochure have a positive effect on the conversation?

- Was there a good, logical flow to the discussion?

Engagement

- Does the conversation pique the attendee's interest?

- Are those listening responding positively?

- Are they being encouraged to connect to the organization to find out more?

- Were all their questions answered?

Reach

- Are the face-to-face meetings helping to acquire new potential donors?

- Are you seeking feedback?

- Are you seeking for ways to improve your performance?

The Pros and Cons

Examining the pros and cons of a new undertaking is always helpful. Review the pluses and minuses before taking on an additional venture.

Pros and Cons of Face-2-face	
Pros	**Cons**
• No real cost	• Requires practice & prep
• More dynamic	• Time consuming
• Creates a stronger relationship	• Not workable for large groups
• Can see body language	• May be tough to keep going on a regular basis
• Increases trust	• Listener may not be attentive
• Most effective	• May be challenge to find mutual times
• Response is immediate	• May be difficult to measure
• Good listening model	

SHOW & TELL

Potential Contacts Worksheet

	A	B	C	D	E	F	G	H
	Person's Nam	Address	Phone	Email Address	Disposition	Attempt 1	Attempt 2	Attempt 3
1								
2	John Doe	123 Main Street Colorado Springs 80905	719-555-1212	johndoe@gmail.com	Appointment set for 9/1/2017 @ 9:30. Coffee at Starbucks	8/5/17	8/25/17	
3								
4								
5								
6								
7								
8								
9								
10								
11								
12								
13								
14								
15								
16								
17								
18								
19								
20								
21								
22								
23								
24								
25								
26								
27								
28								
29								
30								
31								
32								
33								

Download at:

johndleavy.com/PC/PotentialContactsWorksheet.xlsx

SHOW & TELL

Appointment Setting Script Example

Appointment Setting Script Example

Greeting:

Hey Bill...John Calling.

Spend a few minutes finding out what's happening in Bills' life.
Show interest, don't just change the subject.
Be willing to listen if Bill has something to share.

Why You're Calling:

Make sure it's a good time to talk.
If not, ask when you can call back.
Let the person know upfront you're not calling to ask for a gift.
Briefly let them know what God's been up to and how it's affecting you.
Describe what you're working on.

The goal of this call is to set an appointment to meet NOT to get a gift.

Set an Appointment:

Ask if you can meet with them for a cup of coffee or lunch if they have time.

Tell them the appointment time will last no longer than 30 minutes.
Expand on what God's been up to and how it's affecting you.
Give more details about how you're involved.

If the answer is no:
If they don't have time to meet or would rather not meet...ask if they would be willing to receive periodic emails from you and if they would be willing to pray about what you're involved in.
(Don't just start sending them information unless they say yes.)

Confirm the Appointment Details:

Confirm what's been agreed upon. The location, date and time.

Thank them for their willingness to meet.

Show excitement at the prospect of meeting.

Copyright © 2017 Project.Caleb

Download at:

johndleavy.com/PC/AppointmentSettingScriptExample.pdf

SHOW & TELL

Appointment Setting Script Worksheet

Appointment Setting Script Worksheet

Greeting: _____
_____
_____

Why you're calling: _____
_____
_____

Set an Appointment: _____
_____
_____

If the answer is no: _____
_____
_____
_____

Close: (details, clear, directions, date, time)_____
_____
_____
_____
_____
_____

Copyright © 2017 Project.Caleb

Download at:

johndleavy.com/PC/AppointmentSettingScriptWorksheet.pdf

SHOW & TELL

Information Card Example

Name: _____

Phone: _____

Email: _____

What interests the person most? _____
_____
_____

Add you to our mailing list? Yes _____ No _____ Next Contact Date: _____

Comments:
_____
_____
_____
_____
_____
_____
_____
_____

Download at:

johndleavy.com/PC/InformationCardExample.pdf

Donor Card Example

Play a Role in Sponsoring 230 Orphans ($96,600) for 2018

Name: _____

Phone: _____

Email: _____

☐ 1 child @ $35/per month   ☐ _____ Number of children @ $35 per month
☐ One-time gift   ☐ Please contact me by _____ email,_____ phone

Peaceful River Ministries
123 Main Street
Anywhere, USA
Peacefulriver.org

Download at:

johndleavy.com/PC/DonorCardExample.docx

SHOW & TELL

Face-to-face Meeting Script Example (1)

Face-to-face Meeting Script Example

Name: John Doe

Phone: 719-555-1212

Email: John@website.com

Relationship: Friend of Bill P.

Meeting Date/Time: 8/28 @ 9:00 Place: Starbucks on Centennial

Talk about your spiritual journey, how you got to where you are today:

Hearing God's Call...

After leaving Egypt and a series of Red Sea pillar of fire events, the Israelites found themselves on the banks of the Jordan River opposite the Promised Land which God said flows with milk and honey. Moses dispatches twelve trusted spies that included Aaron and Caleb to survey the land. Upon their return, the intelligence reports were good and bad. Yes, the land flowed with milk and honey. God was right. But, the people of the land were strong, the cities were large and well-fortified, and moreover, the descendants of Anak, giants, lived there.

The hearts of the Israelites fell. As they started to murmur and complain to Moses, Caleb stepped forwarded, quieted the crowd and proclaimed: "Let's go up and take the land—now. We can do it." Numbers 13:30 (MSG)

There is much that can be learned from this brief glimpse into history:

- *The people stopped at the banks of the Jordan River*
- *No one rushed ahead into the unknown*
- *A plan was devised and put into action*
- *Valuable intelligence was gathered*
- *The information was weighed and considered*
- *The unbelieving souls, missed their reward and wandered aimlessly*
- *Those that relied upon God's promises "took the land"*

Just as in those days, we'll all run into naysayers more than willing to try and talk us out of a calling we believe is from the same God Caleb served.

Project:Caleb exists to assist groups and organizations in devising a plan, gathering the intelligence, weighting the findings, developing an action plan and "taking the land" which God has called one to conquer.

Talk about the ministries purpose (what's the problem, what's the solution, why you, and why now?)

Copyright © 2017 Project:Caleb

Download at:

johndleavy.com/PC/Face-to-faceMeetingScriptExample.pdf

SHOW &TELL

Face-to-face Meeting Script Example (2)

Why this need?

Those involved in ministry want to spend as much time with these activities as possible and rightfully so. These same people are however not that experienced with the planning, marketing and fundraising chores that go hand-and-hand with ministry. To help these project managers succeed it makes sense for Project:Caleb to shore up these gaps in experiencer by offering coaching and educational services.

Why this way?

Project:Caleb offers it services in a variety of ways for several reasons. First, those heading up the projects come from varied backgrounds and have different experience levels and skills. These same project managers are also dispersed across the country and around the world. To be as practical as possible, Project:Caleb offers its services in-person, over the phone or by Internet facilities such as SKYPE and Go-To-Meeting.

Why us?

Project:Caleb has more than 30 years of experience building businesses along with more than 50 years in technology. John has authored 13 books and taught hundreds of workshops and seminars. He has designed and developed training programs used worldwide. He also has more than 30 years of experience launching and working with non-profits and ministries as well as 15 years of board experience – mostly as chairman of the board and president of past organizations.

Why now?

There is no better time to preach Jesus than now. The projects in New Horizons and Joy to the World Foundations are working hard to accomplish God's leading in a variety of ways from healthcare to education and spiritual development to dignity of life issues and desperately need assistance in the areas of planning, marketing, fundraising and donor development. Project:Caleb is well-prepared to aid in these areas.

Ask if they would be willing to consider ways they might be involved—mention how others are helping.

Close with a final thought.
Ask if you can check back with them in 7 to 10 days—ask if they prefer an email or phone call.

Need to check back on September 2, 2017 by email.

Thank them for listening.

Copyright © 2017 Project:Caleb

Download at:

johndleavy.com/PC/Face-to-faceMeetingScriptExample.pdf

SHOW & TELL

Face-to-face Meeting Script Example (3)

Meeting Comments:

John was very receptive. He's interested in hearing more after he has some time to consider how he might be involved. Need to send second brochure for him to give to a friend.

_____

_____

_____

_____

_____

_____

_____

_____

_____

Copyright © 2017 Project:Caleb

Download at:

johndleavy.com/PC/Face-to-faceMeetingScriptExample.pdf

SHOW & TELL

Face-to-face Meeting Script Worksheet (1)

Face-to-face Meeting Script Worksheet

Name: _____

Phone: _____

Email: _____

Relationship: _____

Meeting Date/Time: _____ Place: _____

Talk about your spiritual journey, how you got to where you are today:

_____

_____

_____

Talk about the ministries purpose (what's the problem, what's the solution, why you, and why now?)

The Problem: _____

_____

The Solution: _____

_____

Why You? _____

_____

Why Now? _____

_____

Ask if they would be willing to consider ways they might be involved—mention how others are helping.

Close with a final thought.
Ask if you can check back with them in 7 to 10 days—ask if they prefer an email or phone call.

_____

Thank them for listening.

Copyright © 2017 Project:Caleb

Download at:

johndleavy.com/PC/Face-to-faceMeetingScriptWorksheet.docx

SHOW & TELL

Face-to-face Meeting Script Worksheet (2)

Meeting Comments:

_____
_____
_____
_____
_____
_____
_____
_____

Copyright © 2017 Project:Caleb

Download at:

johndleavy.com/PC/Face-to-faceMeetingScriptWorksheet.pdf

TEN

Create **AMAZING**
Photos

W hen we talk about including "hero" photos in communications with supporters, we're not referring to images of Superman, Wonder Woman, Spider-Man, or others from the Marvel Universe.

The hero photos we're focusing on are aesthetically pleasing to the eye, conveying emotion, passion, progress being made, lives being changed—positive results being accrued.

Let's look at two examples:

Here's a photo shot of a Haitian child. It certainly expresses love, concern, caring, safety, and the immediate need for assistance.

Here's a second photo of a child in need—possibly? There's no way to know. It's a great photo of a young girl. But what's her story?

The composition of "hero" photos needs to tell a story—transmit a message.

👍 **Students lined up, standing poised in front of their school building, convey what?**

Students at play during recess show they're having fun. Life is good.

Students receiving packages during the Christmas holidays or lining up to receive new school uniforms tell a great story of caring for the less fortunate.

👍 Photos need to show ministry in action.

Some mechanical photo issues need to be attended to as well:

- The resolution of the photo needs to be high enough so that the image appears clear and sharp.

- The photo should load quickly, whether being viewed on a website or a mobile device.

- The color balance should be correct, so the primary colors appear as intended.

- What's going on in the photo should be obvious. If not, add a caption to help the viewer understand the image.

The file size of photos taken with a smartphone is quite large, usually several megabytes. Photos uploaded to websites or blogs should be much smaller in size. Software like Photoshop should be used to prepare the photo for the Internet. Images that load slowly on websites or blogs often cause users to exit the site and visit elsewhere.

Choose your photos wisely. Seek help from a friend or professional if necessary.

To recap, here are a few tips when considering a photo:

- **Photos need a purpose.** Don't snap pictures without considering how they might be used later. Resist using images as fillers for space.

- **Capture an emotion.** Photos are used to tell a story or add to one already underway. Photos connect people to what's happening even though the action may be miles away.

- **Don't forget people.** Photos of people boost conversion by 95%. People relate to other human beings.

- **Prioritize photo quality.** You don't have to be a Photoshop expert to know when you see a photo of poor quality.

- **Match the photo to the mood.** Make sure the photo appeals to the target audience. Take care to ensure the image aligns with the style and tone of what's being used.

- **Hold the haphazard photos.** Avoid using cheesy images. Today's audiences are quite discerning.

The Pros and Cons

Here's a quick list of pros and cons.

Pros and Cons of Photos	
Pros	**Cons**
• No real cost	• Requires practice & prep
• Tells a better story	• Maybe time consuming
• Draws in the reader	• Takes forethought
• No longer any developing costs w/smartphones	• Composition is everything
• Creates a strong emotion	• May be challenge at times
• Low-cost editing solutions	• Can't do everything by yourself
	• Results may be hard to measure

ELEVEN
(8 MIN READ)

Create **AMAZING** Communication Plans

I f we boil down a communication plan, it's really nothing more than deciding what to say, to whom, when, and by what means. There's a goal component, as we want the communication that takes place between the organization and individuals to generate some sort of action.

In the following discussion, nine ingredients are outlined in developing and executing a communication plan that produces positive results:

1. Take stock of your current situation – Includes three parts: identifying where you are today, securing the necessary skills, people, and resources, and determining the goals. It's always good to take stock of the current situation. What needs changing or improving? As the organization moves forward, what's next? What are the

problems we can tackle in the coming year? Make a short list and prioritize the items. The next operation involves taking inventory of the necessary skills available, the people on board, and the resources still accessible. What's on hand will undoubtedly factor into what can be accomplished in the coming year. The last element is the goals. What goals can the group set that are relatively certain to be attainable? Keep in mind that the goals should align with the organization's vision and mission.

2. **Define the target audiences** – Identify the ideal prospects and segment the audience types. One of the key components of any communication plan is identifying the ideal donors who should receive the pending message. Sending a message to thousands of random email addresses is ineffective. Don't think surely some will be receptive. An organization needs to understand its potential supporters and the channels they use for information. Is the audience under 35 or older than 55? Are there more women than men? Are they passionate about orphans or drilling wells for farming? Are they retired or still working? Do they prefer to receive newsletters via the US Mail or email? Do they congregate on social channels such as Facebook, Snapchat, or Instagram? Audiences need to be segmented based on some "ideal" criteria.

3. **Develop the messaging** – Tell a compelling story and tailor it to reflect the target audience. A good story always includes a hook. Herman Melville used "Call me Ishmael" in Moby-Dick. JK Rowling started Harry Potter and the Sorcerer's Stone with "Mr. and Mrs. Dursley, of number four, Privet Drive, were proud to say that they were perfectly normal, thank you very much." Of course, there's George Lucas' Episode IV – A New Hope that begins with "A long time ago in a galaxy far, far away…". Every great story starts with the hook. These stories also include problems that need to be solved, passion from those wanting to eliminate the issue, and real names and places. Keep the story short and do not ramble. Find ways that allow the reader to see themselves in the situation. Discuss the benefits one receives once the solution is applied, as well as what happens if no one comes to assist. If you'll be talking to multiple generations or audiences with varying views, then the messaging needs to be crafted in line with how they see things. What's important to them? What are they passionate about regarding the work the organization is currently undertaking? The same message will not resonate with everyone.

4. **Select the communication tactics** – Several things factor into deciding which tactics may work best: budget, available skills and know-how, time, and audience segments (those receiving the communication). Over the

airwaves (or the Internet) and on the street are also aspects. Younger generations expect social contacts to be brief. They'll also prefer sound and video over written words. The more mature crowd is more comfortable with printed materials. Choose the communication channels wisely. Go with their preferences and not your own. Decisions need to be made regarding whether the communication is passive, such as a newsletter, or a social channel where engagement can occur. Preparing the actual marketing pieces is the last item in this category. Printing and mailing materials can be expensive, so choose your communication methods carefully.

Did you know?
Sending out a postcard cultivation to donors produced a **204%** increase in their year-end giving. (NextAfter.com Experiment #6404)

5. **Plan for two-way communication** – Two-way communication needs to be decided on a case-by-case basis. Some social channels may be appropriate while others may not. Audience age also factors into whether social channels are employed. A newsletter is a static method of communication, while social channels allow engagement. The organization needs to decide at what point they want the audience members to chime in on what's being said. Social metrics need to be determined in advance. Some metrics will be more important and

meaningful than others. Yes, it's good that people "like" the organization's Facebook page, but those who subscribe to the organization's newsletter, click through and visit the website, and give a gift are more valuable.

6. **Establish your time frame** – Establishing what will be done when is essential to the success of any communication plan. A newsletter sent out when those in charge have time does not bode well for growing the readership. People expect things to happen at regular, predictable intervals. The Sunday paper comes out on Saturday night. Mail is delivered each day within a specific time window. Be consistent. The readership will settle into your schedule, come what may, if your delivery is predictable. Timing is also crucial when determining when to initiate a communication plan. The year-end plea should begin to be discussed as the fall starts, not in December. When using social media, the channel being used determines the communication schedule. Communicating on Facebook once a month or uploading month-old photos to Instagram will fail to garner people's attention. Depending on the audience, postings to Facebook may need to occur several times a day for several days or more than once a week. It depends on what's being accomplished. The "Insta" in Instagram stands for instantly. People use this channel to share what's happening now. Ensure the communication

schedule aligns with the channels being used.

7. **Draft a budget** – "What can we afford?" is always an all-important question during any planning process. Funding the communication plan may be the determining factor in what gets approved. You'll need to strike a balance between maximizing the value of the dollars allocated. If you're unsure of what the communication effort may produce, then start small. Prototype a few communication choices to see what results can be generated. Once you're sure of a direction, then more money can be allocated.

8. **Execute the plan** – Tuning up the resources and assigning responsibilities are essential in any project plan. Making sure the necessary resources are in place and ready to go determines the viability of any communication plan. The resources may include people, skills, marketing materials, and communication choices. Everyone knowing their role in the communication strategy is crucial. to success or failure. The management of resources also plays a significant role in the project's success.

Monitor the results and adjust – Determine the reporting methods and adjusting helps guarantee the plan's success. Take the time to understand what the numbers really mean to the project and record those that are most meaningful. Yes. It's important to note that 2,000 email newsletters were sent out. But it's more vital to know that only 560 were opened. If the numbers are not producing the desired results, then the communication method may need to be adjusted or turned off, and an alternative communication avenue chosen. Be flexible and monitor things closely.

This chapter concludes with examples of two communication schedules, one that runs year-round and breaks down the communication by donor (one-time, monthly, major giver, and another that is seasonal.) The second schedule looks at the communication tasks by channel. Build it whichever way suits you.

Find two Communication Plans at the end of this chapter.

Feel free to delete or add donor segments or tasks to make the communication plan simpler or more complex as needed.

The Pros and Cons

Review this list of pros and cons before implementing the communication plan.

Pros and Cons of a Communication Plan	
Pros	**Cons**
• Promotes community	• Requires practice & prep
• Builds trust	• Can't be haphazard
• Can create a two-way communication channel	• Takes time and resources
	• Composition is everything
• No longer any developing costs w/smartphones	• Must have a purpose
	• Channel needs to match recipient
• Creates a personal touch	
• Gives the recipient insight into the organization	• At time, results may be hard to measure

SHOW & TELL

Communication Plan by Donor Schedule Example (1)

Sample Communication Plan
By Donor Schedule

Here's what a yearly schedule might look like when communicating with all three donor types. Let's say the three groups all start giving in January.

January
One-time Gift   Immediate
Email tax deductible receipt sent by email.
Within 24 Hours
Personalized email thanking the person and highlight the gift's impact.

Monthly Gift   Immediate
Email tax deductible receipt sent by email.
Within 24 Hours
Phone call is possible thanking the person and highlight the gift's impact.

Major Donor   Immediate
Email tax deductible receipt sent by email.
Within 24 Hours
Phone call thanking the person and highlight the gift's impact.

February
One-time Gift   Personalized email highlighting their gift and the project's impact.
Monthly Gift   Personalized email highlighting their gift and the project's impact.
Major Gift   Phone calls highlighting their gift and the project's impact. Followed up by email with details of the phone call.
Phone call telling another donor's story on how supporting the project is changing their life. Followed up by email with details of the phone call.

March
One-time Gift   Personalized email telling another donor's story on how supporting the project is changing their life. Ask for a second gift.
Monthly Gift   Personalized email telling another donor's story on how supporting the project is changing their life.
Major Gift   Phone calls highlighting their gift and the project's impact. Followed up by email with details of the phone call.
Major Gift   Phone call telling another donor's story on how supporting the project is changing their life. Followed up by email with details of the phone call.

April
Monthly Gift   Personalized email highlighting their gift and the project's impact.
Monthly Gift   Email newsletter recap of past successes and needs.

Copyright © 2017 Project:Caleb

Download at:

johndleavy.com/PC/CommunicationPlanDonorSchedule.pdf

SHOW & TELL

Communication Plan by Donor Schedule Example (2)

Sample Communication Plan
By Donor Schedule

Major Gift	Phone calls highlighting their gift and the project's impact. Followed up by email with details of the phone call.
	Phone call telling another donor's story on how supporting the project is changing their life. Followed up by email with details of the phone call.
Major Gift	Email newsletter recap of past successes and needs.
May	
Monthly Gift	Personalized email telling another donor's story on how supporting the project is changing their life.
Major Gift	Phone calls highlighting their gift and the project's impact. Followed up by email with details of the phone call.
	Phone call telling another donor's story on how supporting the project is changing their life. Followed up by email with details of the phone call.
June	
Monthly Gift	Personalized email highlighting their gift and the project's impact.
Major Gift	Phone calls highlighting their gift and the project's impact. Followed up by email with details of the phone call.
	Phone call telling another donor's story on how supporting the project is changing their life. Followed up by email with details of the phone call.
July	
One-time Gift	Personalized email highlighting project's impact.
	Email newsletter recap of past successes and needs.
Monthly Gift	Personalized email telling another donor's story on how supporting the project is changing their life.
Monthly Gift	Email newsletter recap of past successes and needs.
Major Gift	Phone calls highlighting their gift and the project's impact. Followed up by email with details of the phone call.
	Phone call telling another donor's story on how supporting the project is changing their life. Followed up by email with details of the phone call.
Major Gift	Email newsletter recap of past successes and needs.
August	
Monthly Gift	Personalized email highlighting their gift and the project's impact.
Major Gift	Phone calls highlighting their gift and the project's impact. Followed up by email with details of the phone call.
	Phone call telling another donor's story on how supporting the project is changing their life. Followed up by email with details of the phone call.

Copyright © 2017 ProjectCeleb

Download at:

johndleavy.com/PC/CommunicationPlanDonorSchedule.pdf

SHOW & TELL

Communication Plan by Donor Schedule Example (3)

Sample Communication Plan
By Donor Schedule

September
Monthly Gift — Personalized email telling another donor's story on how supporting the project is changing their life.

Major Gift — Phone calls highlighting their gift and the project's impact. Followed up by email with details of the phone call.
Phone call telling another donor's story on how supporting the project is changing their life. Followed up by email with details of the phone call.

October
One-time Gift — Personalized email highlighting project's impact.
Email newsletter recap of past successes and needs.
Monthly Gift — Personalized email highlighting their gift and the project's impact.
Monthly Gift — Email newsletter recap of past successes and needs.
Major Gift — Phone calls highlighting their gift and the project's impact. Followed up by email with details of the phone call.
Phone call telling another donor's story on how supporting the project is changing their life. Followed up by email with details of the phone call.

Major Gift — Email newsletter recap of past successes and needs.
November
One-time Gift — See Sample EOY Communication Plan Schedule.
Monthly Gift — See Sample EOY Communication Plan Schedule.
Major Gift — See Sample EOY Communication Plan Schedule.
December
One-time Gift — See Sample EOY Communication Plan Schedule.
Monthly Gift — See Sample EOY Communication Plan Schedule.
Major Gift — See Sample EOY Communication Plan Schedule.

Copyright © 2017 Project:Caleb

Download at:

johndleavy.com/PC/CommunicationPlanDonorSchedule.pdf

SHOW & TELL

Communication Plan by Channel Example (1)

Sample Year-long Communication Plan
Schedule – January through September

Make the communication touches brief, concise and to the point. The newsletter should be a page or less. The blog and social media posts should be no more than 25 to 100 words. The Email recap should be short, perhaps a half-page.

January
Newsletter	Week 1 – Highlight project progress, lives being changed, individual's stories
Blog	Weeks 2 and 3 – post what's happening, develop a story line
Social Media	Weekly – one or two posts telling what's happening
Email	Week 4 – Recap newsletter highlights, blog and social media posts
Support Letter	Week 4 – Recap progress made, impact, challenges overcome, obstacles, financial support needed

February
Newsletter	Week 1 – Highlight project progress, lives being changed, individual's stories
Blog	Weeks 2 and 3 – post what's happening, develop a story line
Social Media	Weekly – one or two posts telling what's happening
Email	Week 4 – Recap newsletter highlights, blog and social media posts
Support Letter	Week 4 – Recap progress made, impact, challenges overcome, obstacles, financial support needed

March
Newsletter	Week 1 – Highlight project progress, lives being changed, individual's stories
Blog	Weeks 2 and 3 – post what's happening, develop a story line
Social Media	Weekly – one or two posts telling what's happening
Email	Week 4 – Recap newsletter highlights, blog and social media posts
Support Letter	Week 4 – Recap progress made, impact, challenges overcome, obstacles, financial support needed

April
Newsletter	Week 1 – Highlight project progress, lives being changed, individual's stories
Blog	Weeks 2 and 3 – post what's happening, develop a story line
Social Media	Weekly – one or two posts telling what's happening
Email	Week 4 – Recap newsletter highlights, blog and social media posts
Support Letter	Week 4 – Recap progress made, impact, challenges overcome, obstacles, financial support needed

May
Newsletter	Week 1 – Highlight project progress, lives being changed, individual's stories
Blog	Weeks 2 and 3 – post what's happening, develop a story line
Social Media	Weekly – one or two posts telling what's happening
Email	Week 4 – Recap newsletter highlights, blog and social media posts
Support Letter	Week 4 – Recap progress made, impact, challenges overcome, obstacles, financial support needed

June
Newsletter	Week 1 – Highlight project progress, lives being changed, individual's stories
Blog	Weeks 2 and 3 – post what's happening, develop a story line

Copyright © 2017 Project Caleb

Download at:

johndleavy.com/PC/CommunicationPlanChannel.pdf

SHOW & TELL

Communication Plan by Channel Example (2)

Social Media	Weekly – one or two posts telling what's happening
Email	Week 4 – Recap newsletter highlights, blog and social media posts
Support Letter	Week 4 – Recap progress made, impact, challenges overcome, obstacles, financial support needed
July	
Newsletter	Week 1 – Highlight project progress, lives being changed, individual's stories
Blog	Weeks 2 and 3 – post what's happening, develop a story line
Social Media	Weekly – one or two posts telling what's happening
Email	Week 4 – Recap newsletter highlights, blog and social media posts
Support letter	Week 4 – Recap progress made, impact, challenges overcome, obstacles, financial support needed
August	
Newsletter	Week 1 – Highlight project progress, lives being changed, individual's stories
Blog	Weeks 2 and 3 – post what's happening, develop a story line
Social Media	Weekly – one or two posts telling what's happening
Email	Week 4 – Recap newsletter highlights, blog and social media posts
Support Letter	Week 4 – Recap progress made, impact, challenges overcome, obstacles, financial support needed
September	
Newsletter	Week 1 – Highlight project progress, lives being changed, individual's stories
Blog	Weeks 2 and 3 – post what's happening, develop a story line
Social Media	Weekly – one or two posts telling what's happening
Email	Week 4 – Recap newsletter highlights, blog and social media posts
Support Letter	Week 4 – Recap progress made, impact, challenges overcome, obstacles, financial support needed

Suspend regular communication schedule and shift to EOY plan

October	
Email	Week 2 – Send out warmup announcement the EOY theme
Blog	Week 3 – Post story about impact made during the year
Social Media	Week 3 – Create Facebook post linking to Donate page
November	
Email	Week 1 – Continue to show impact/immediate needs
	Week 1 – Announce GivingTuesday campaign
	Week 3 – Hold GivingTuesday event
	Week 4 – Thank people for participating in GivingTuesday
Blog	Week 2 – Post story about impact made during the year
	Week 3 – Post story about impact made during the year
	Week 3 – Hold GivingTuesday event
	Week 4 – Thank people for participating in GivingTuesday
Social Media	Week 3 – Continue GivingTuesday campaign
	Week 3 – Hold GivingTuesday event
	Week 4 – Thank people for participating in GivingTuesday
December	

Copyright © 2017 Project:Caleb

Download at:

johndleavy.com/PC/CommunicationPlanChannel.pdf

SHOW & TELL

Communication Plan by Channel Example (3)

Email	Week 1 – Send out EOY email talking about successes
	Week 2 – Send out EOY email asking for donation/talking about needs
	Week 3 – Send out EOY email asking for donation/ talking about impact
	Week 4 – Send out "Time is running out" EOY email
Blog	Week 1 – Post story about impact
	Week 2 – Post story about impact
	Week 3 – Post story about impact
	Week 4 – Post story about impact
Social Media	Week 1 – Create Facebook post linking to Donate page
	Week 2 – Create Facebook post linking to Donate page
	Week 3 – Create Facebook post linking to Donate page
	Week 3 – Create Facebook post linking to Donate page
January	
Email	Week 1 – Thank donors/talking about successes
Blog	Week 1 – Thank donors/talking about successes
Social Media	Week 1 – Thank donors/talking about successes

Copyright © 2017 Project Caleb

Download at:

johndleavy.com/PC/CommunicationPlanChannel.pdf

TWELVE

(10 MIN READ)

What's Working—
What's Not

A s you begin conversing with potential supporters and donors, some of the communication avenues you choose will be effective while others will not. This chapter explores the possible reasons why success may be elusive.

This section starts out listing some common reasons the communication may be failing, no matter which channel was chosen:

- Were goals defined before starting? Were the goals motivating? Were they in line with your mission? Were they aligned with donor expectations?

- Were the audiences segmented so that everyone received the same message?

- Was the communication plan adhered to?

- Were the stories great?

- Were new donors always welcomed?

- Was value always provided?

- Were there always clear calls-to-action?

- Was the content compelling?

- Were "hero" photos used?

- Was planning a second thought?

- Were the messages donor-centric?

- Were the communication methods aligned with how constituents converse?

- Was every message grammar-checked and spell-checked?

- Were comments responded to quickly?

- Did you enjoy yourself?

Now, let's drill down into each of the various communication methods to see if specific issues were preventing success:

Website's Not Working

- Is the website mobile-friendly?

- Was it designed by a professional?

> *"**Forget the brother-in-law connection**—have the website done by a professional."*

- Was it appropriately promoted?

- Do the images load quickly?

- Was a maintenance schedule put in place?

- Was the content reviewed regularly, and were the links tested?

- Was someone put in charge of administering the site?

- Was the site launched and forgotten about?

- Were different messages constructed for the various visitor segments?

- Were eye-pleasing colors and fonts chosen to enhance the visitor experience?

- Do visitors know what to do once they reach the site?

- Was the target audience well-defined?

Blog's Not Working

- Was there a lack of passion?

- Did severe blogger's block creep in?

- Did the site lack personality?

- Was the content engaging?

- Were open-ended or thought-provoking questions asked to get the readership involved?

- Is there anything that sets the blog apart from every other one?

> **"*Blogs build community—*** *tell don't sell."*

- Are outside experts ever asked to contribute their expertise?

- Is the blog difficult to share?

- Are readers given a reason to return?

Email Messages Not Working

- Were too few emails sent out to gauge success?

- Was an email automation marketing system, such as Mailchimp, used to track results?

  *"**Remember, you're writing to a friend**—not someone on a call sheet."*

- Were the email lists cleaned before starting?

- Was personalizing the messages ignored?

- Were the emails optimized for mobile devices?

- Were people allowed to opt in?

- Were the messages sent out at the optimum times?

- Were the messages too long?

- Was the purpose of the message clear and concise?

Newsletters Not Working

- Was the content and readership in sync?

  "Use the newsletter as an opportunity to build relationships."

- Was external content linked to so readers could go deeper?

- Were readers encouraged to engage?

- Was the newsletter more self-promotional and less helpful?

- Was the structure and flow easy to follow?

- Did the headings draw the readers into the stories?

- Did the content stay true to the organization's mission?

- Was the newsletter too lengthily?

- Were the newsletters sent as an attachment?

Appeal Letters Not Working

- Did the appeal ever reach its purpose?

> "**Don't tell a great story**—and forget the appeal."

- Did the appeal raise more questions than it answered?

- Was the donation page easy to navigate?

- Did the appeal lack a clear call to action?

- Was it obvious how the funds are being spent?

- Was the focus on impact and not fundraising?

- Are the appeal letters sent out on an irregular basis?

- Were impactful stories shared?

- Did "the ask" come before the relationship was built?

- Was the giving ability of donors gauged beforehand?

- Were compelling videos used?

- Were donors afforded different giving options?

Brochure's Not Working

- Was the brochure done by a professional?

- Did the brochure include a fair amount of white space?

> **"Does the brochure standout**—is it a keeper?"

- Was a follow-up done on the brochures?

- Was jargon and "church-speak" left out?

- Did the brochure focus on what the reader needs to know and not what the organization wants to tell them?

- Did the brochure stand out from all the others?

- Did it answer the "who", "what", "when", "where", and "why" questions?

- Was the brochure all flash and no facts?

Presentations Not Working

- Were a reasonable number of slides used (10 to 12)?

> **"Great presentations don't just happen**—they require practice, practice, practice."

- Were the colors and fonts visually pleasing?

- Did the presentation run too long?

- Was the presentation given to the right person(s)?

- Was there a summary at the end?

- Was there too much staring at the screen and not enough looking at the potential supporter?

- Was too much animation employed?

- Were the slides cluttered?

Face-to-face Meetings Not Working

- Was there a sense of poor rapport?

> **"Remember, you're the messenger**—you speak for those in need."

- Was there a lack of eye contact?

- Did the conversations lack direction?

- Was a script used to stay on track?

- Was there a lack of energy?

- Was there a failure to understand the other person?

- Was there poor preparation?

- Was little passion shared?

- Was the presentation from the wrong point of view, yours or theirs?

- Was there anything unique about the organization that was shared?

- Was there a lack of rehearsal?

Work on answering the questions that relate to the problem in communication areas, and you'll be well on your way to better success.

About the Author

John founded ministryTHRIVE in 2018. Its mission: "*Provide exceptional learning experiences to those in ministry to ensure they master the skills necessary to achieve their goals.*"

ministryTHRIVE plans to develop and deliver learning materials in eight critical areas of non-profit success: administration, management, branding, marketing, communication, engagement, fundraising, and donor relations. Initially, the educational materials will take the form of articles, eBooks, paperbacks, podcasts, and webinars.

Before ministryTHRIVE, John founded InPlainSite Marketing, a leader in developing and delivering digital marketing strategies. John consulted and presented to Fortune 50 and 100 companies. He is a bestselling author of eighteen books. *Ignite Your Email Campaign* is available on Amazon.com and at bookstores worldwide. His books have been featured in Amazon's Top 10 in the US, Canada, the UK, and Australia. John's musings are regularly picked up by CustomerThink.com, Business2Community.com, TheStreet.com, Entrepreneur.com, Visa Business, *Yahoo!* Finance, MSNBC.com, The Globe and Mail, Reuters, and The New York Daily News.

John has served on the boards of numerous non-profits for over a dozen years. He has enjoyed leading as either president, chairman of the board, or director, doing what he can to help organizations succeed. He has also valued his time as a volunteer in the trenches.

As president and chairman of the board, John has helped launch a crisis pregnancy center and thrift shop while living in Illinois. In Colorado, he was asked to serve as president and chairman of the board for a Christian startup school in Woodland Park. He has also served as a director on the board of Middle Market Entrepreneurs, an entrepreneurial organization based in Colorado Springs. He has served on a leadership council, as creative director, and in various capacities as a church volunteer. John believes his most rewarding times as a volunteer are when he gets to work alongside Kay or one of their children or grandchildren. Today, John's life centers on God, family, church, and community.

John loves spending time with Kay, his bride and best friend of 48 years of marriage. They have three of the greatest kids, okay, grownups, on this planet, as well as eight grandchildren. John and Kay live in Colorado.

Other books by John D. Leavy:

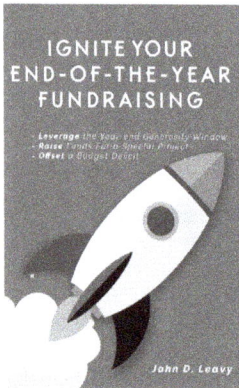

"Ignite Your End-of-the-Year Fundraising" is a practical guide to help you set clear goals, attract new donors, tell better stories, and manage your fundraising plan with confidence. Written for beginners, stalled organizations, and seasoned fundraisers alike, it turns a stressful process into a focused, effective, and rewarding one—without the jargon.

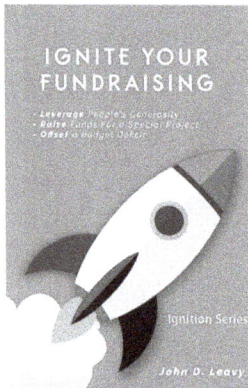

"Ignite Your Fundraising" is a clear, practical guide that takes the stress out of raising support. You'll learn how to set realistic goals, reach new donors, tell stories that inspire, and manage your plan from start to finish. Whether you're new to fundraising, starting over, or ready to grow, it gives you the tools and confidence to raise more—and make a lasting impact.

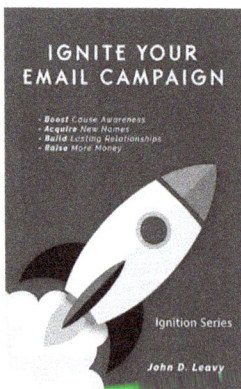

"Ignite Your Email Campaign" is a practical guide for ministries and nonprofits that want to use email more effectively. It walks you through how to raise awareness for your cause, grow your audience, build lasting relationships, and increase donations—all through clear, repeatable strategies. Whether you're starting fresh or refining what you already do, this book helps you turn every email into meaningful connection and measurable impact.

STARTING A

The Roadmap to Building a Thriving, Sustainable Ministry

MINISTRY

2nd Edition

John D. Leavy

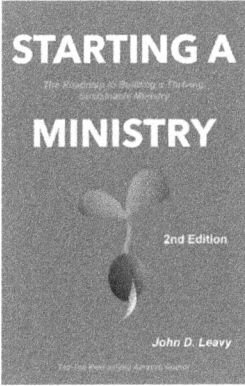

"**Starting a Ministry**" is a down-to-earth guide that helps new ministry leaders cut through the stress, fear, and confusion that often come with getting started. It lays out a clear, step-by-step path—what to do first, what to do next—so you can build on a solid foundation. From organization and planning to fundraising and growth, it gives you the tools to create a strong, sustainable ministry that lasts. **REVISED: July 2024**.

Available at Amazon.com
or wherever books are sold.

....

www.ingramcontent.com/pod-product-compliance
Lightning Source LLC
Chambersburg PA
CBHW071657200326
41519CB00012BA/2542